Enoteca

Thanks are due to
Giovanni Brachetti Montorselli
and the editing staff of the
Consorzio del Marchio Storico Chianti Classico

Conceived by: Ennio Bazzoni
Texts: Maria Salemi
Translation: Gretchen Harrison Trevisan,
Anthony Brierley

Editing: Alissa Zavanella
with the contribution of Lucia Franciosi
Design: Francesco Bertini

Map: Giancarlo Ferraris
Photos: Lorenzo Bojola,
Archivio Consorzio del Marchio Storico Chianti Classico,
Giuliano Valsecchi, Archivio Nardini Editore

Technical coordination: Paola Bianchi
Colour reproductions: Fotolito Toscana, Firenze

www.nardinieditore.it

Maria Salemi

Chianti
Classico

Legend, history and quality of the prince of the table, the symbol of a land

NARDINI EDITORE

Among vineyards and castles

The area of Chianti is a land of hard, rocky earth, a land of limestone and clay, galestro and alberese stone; who can say why forests, gardens, vines, olives and fig trees spring from the thin layer of fertile soil above this rock. A land of undulating hills and knolls, with roads and paths that wind around and over them, with farms and walled villas, abbeys and parish churches, castles and crumbling towers, stone villages and austere houses. This is Chianti. A land of feuds between Siena and Arezzo, and between Florence and Siena, a land of ancient, allusive names, rich in mystery and imagination, vivifying the landscapes of 14th-century Sienese paint-

ings; a land of warriors and saints, of navigators and artists, of peasants and noblemen; a land that shines through Bertolucci's camera lens in the sunny noontides of *Stealing Beauty*; a land to drink in, to inhale, to savour with all the senses – Chianti.

A land of wine. Noble, elegant, heart-warming, healthy; wine to enjoy – in the past made from just-crushed grapes, now aged – together with simple, genuine Tuscan food. Wine which only in conformity with the strictest rules has the right to call itself by the name of the land from which it springs and with which it shares a long and turbulent history.

Set in the midst of austere cypresses, Badia a Passignano still has the look of a fortified village with high defense walls.

"The most moving landscape in the world"

This definition, conceived and written for Tuscany, seems to be inspired by the Chianti of those who understand its secret rhythms and mysterious dynamics, who see beyond the undulating lines of the horizon, the clear colours, the bright sky, and the landscape dotted with evidence of human work. Admiring the beauty of its landscape means reviewing the history of the people and of the events that have made it so. The vines, the cypresses and the olive trees, more than the forests of ilex, oak, black hornbeam and chestnut, really seem to be the eternal protagonists of the landscape of the Chianti area as it is known today. And yet, until the 7th-6th century BC there was a long period of time during which neither the vine branches of Dionysus nor the silvery tree of Athena, nor the sombre banner of Attis or Adonis characterized the hills. What changed its rugged aspect was Roman colonization, whose application of order, rationality and normalization gave the territory a different appearance, measuring it, redistributing it and uniting it with a road network to the rest of the empire. And although during the early Middle Ages it returned to its wild state, from the middle of the 11th century to the beginning of the 14th century, there began that gradual creation of the present landscape that has quite legitimately been called a work of art.

The new aesthetic balance reflected the new social balance, with a city-based ruling class and a class of landlords tied to the economic activities of the land, a land no longer "natural" and wild, but dotted with castles, rural hamlets, "houses of the gentry" and "of the workers," parish churches and abbeys that bore witness to an intense human presence as would never be seen again in this area. Not, at least, after the Black Death, which raged throughout Europe in the middle of the 14th century, decimating its population. Not after the gradual disappearance of small properties owned by farmers and city dwellers, testified by the passage of old "case da signore" to rural dwellings. But not even after the "refeudalization" of the 15th and 16th centuries, or the agricultur-

The dark patch of a cypress grove, harmoniously set into the wooded landscape of Chianti.

Leopoldine farmhouse: a tower-shaped central element rises above the lower body of the building.

al revival of the 18th century, or the 19th-century explosion of new fields, with their rows of vines, olive trees and fruit trees, and the centralization in villa-farms of the transformation and commercialization of products in response to market demands.

Chianti is not gentle, nor is the profile of her hills rounded, at least not in that "historic" area which as we shall see corresponds to the present communes of Castellina, Gaiole and Radda, which becomes gentler only toward Berardenga to the south, and to the north, in the valleys of the Greve and Pesa. Nor is it as heavily populated as the Florentine hills.

It is a solitary land, by its very nature unsuitable for agriculture and other economic activities, but one which human labour has succeeded in "domesticating" in the forms we see today. Thus, if the memory of a region abounding in forests, echoing with the noise of gentlemanly hunts and teeming with wild animals, or at any rate animals raised in an untamed state, is now lost, today we can still discover something of its past in the enduring traces of the "podere" which, having developed from ancient settlement patterns

and maturing in the modern age, produced the "mezzadria", or sharecropping system, with its scattered inhabited nuclei and its alternation of cultivated fields, meadows, terraces and forests.

"Case su podere" and "mezzadria"

At the end of the 19th century, and often much earlier, poderi (farms) individually run by sharecroppers became – at Brolio, Meleto, Vicchiomaggio and Uzzano – part of balanced systems of poderi and fattorie (group of farms) belonging to the enlightened bourgeoisie and also to descendants of the ancient landed aristocracy. Yet sharecropping really was the crucial element of the most original and celebrated aspect of the Tuscan landscape in general, and Chianti in particular. Let us take a closer look.

At the end of the Middle Ages, the period in which it started, sharecropping undoubtedly represented a highly advanced form of land management in which the farmer, no longer a servant or slave, shared directly in the profits. The owner, in fact,

provided the farmland, equipped with a house and farming "conveniences" as well as, in all or part, the large livestock, while the farmer contributed the work of his entire family and the technical skills necessary for working the land. If on the one hand there was the obligation to reside there permanently – and thus live in isolation and marginalization, with hard work for the entire family and life at the subsistence level – on the other there was a kind of freedom, a roof for the duration of the contract and daily bread. However, since after the seeds had been deducted the profits were divided in half, the indebtedness of the farmers proved to be inevitable in adverse years and on lands that were less fertile or impoverished due to the absence of owners who benefited from the revenue but refused to reinvest in the land or make any effort to improve it.

Around the "casa su podere", which replaced or accompanied the older pattern of village settlements, the growing of wheat, barley and other grains spread alongside the olive trees, the fruit trees and the vines tied to the live supports of the field maple (*Acer campestris*), separated by low dry-stone walls that were tended as if they were architecture.

This was the hilly agrarian landscape of Chianti, a landscape which due to the abandonment of mixed

A fine example of a vineyard laid out "a rittochino".

farming in the area in the last forty or fifty years, has assumed a variety of particular and characterizing forms. In Chianti, however, the crisis and abandonment of the sharecropping system did not result in the disappearance of the old pattern of scattered farmhouses, villas and fattorie, which – although often stripped of their former agricultural function – have on the contrary been given a new lease of life due to the high environmental value of the territory.

Its lands, on the other hand, have partly lost that picturesque quality that was characteristic of the past, if only for the disappearance of farm livestock. Lands extensively remodelled by the intervention of excavators; such that today their surfaces appear less rugged and broken than they were originally. The old embankments and walls, which especially in the 19th century were made to give farmers flat areas of ground for growing crops, thus interrupting the natural slopes of the hills and breaking the excessively rapid and damaging run-off of rain water, have now been destroyed. The newly-made plots of land are dominated by a geometrical landscape of vine cultivation, with a return to the layout of rows "a rittochino", that is, running in a vertical direction from hill to valley. An organization of the land and of cultivation explained by the need to make tractors and farm machinery work efficiently and safely, while problems of rainwater run-off and erosion are dealt with by modern drainage systems.

The result is a different kind of beauty of vast tracts of the land, with orderly, symmetrical rows of vines cloaking the slopes against the purplish hued hills behind them.

Ancient names

In the heart of Tuscany is a small area of land surrounded by hills, solitary and uncontaminated, with historical roots that date back to as early as the remote Bronze Age evidenced by sources now mute: fossil remains, terracotta fragments, carved stones, weapons and utensils. This is ancient Chianti, whose primeval history is still shrouded in mystery, as is also, in spite of the numerous discov-

eries of tombs and settlements, that of the Etruscan people who dominated the area up until the period of the Roman conquest.

The name of the region has long been the object of conflicting interpretations. The well-known 19th-century geographer Emanuele Repetti claimed that it derived from the Latin verb *clango*, meaning "to resound," a word evoking the noise of those aristocratic hunts which once animated the forests, and in support of this theory he mentioned Avane and Avenano, names which in his view derived from the Latin expression *a venando*, "for hunting." However, etymological marshes can prove treacherous even for the most scrupulous scholars. Thus, even if our territory is mentioned for the first time in a document of the end of the 11th century attesting to the donation in 790 of a farm "in Clanti" to the monks of San Bartolomeo a Ripoli near Florence, it seems that the origin of the name is much older. It is associated with an important Etruscan family, the Clante, commemorated on many funerary inscriptions.

Here, however, all names bear witness to a history of domination: of the Etruscan one above all in those with the suffixes *-na* and *-ne*, including Avane, which may come from Avenal, as Nusenna does from Nuzinai, Rencine from Remzna, Rufena from Rufni and Vercenni from Varcna. The suffixes *-ano* and *-ana* (Uzzano, Sillano, Passignano, Panzano) refer to the Latin world, as do all the names that reflect the military domination of Rome in the subjected lands: Cintora, for example, refers to *centuria*, and Petroio to *praetorium*.

And when the gentlemen of German origin took shelter in the hills here, a flowering of settlements reflected this fact (Monterinaldi, Montebenichi and others), while the agrarian expansion was inspired by the terminology of deforestation and of cultivation (Cetinaia). Names, then, are an indication of a people, of a civilization, of a social reality, with differing characteristics, each distinct from the other, deeply etched in the reality of this land.

With one eye on history...

In the Middle Ages Clante remained isolated, cut off from the great main Roman roads and from the ancient Via Cassia, which followed the eastern slopes of its mountains, barely touching it, preferring instead the upper Valdarno.

The Via Francigena, passing through Siena and Lucca to join Rome to mid-western Europe, went through the nearby Valdelsa.

Yet in spite of this tendency toward isolation, mentions of Chianti crop up in all the documents of the time. They tell us of recurring conflicts, of town rivalries, of wars waged by powerful cities which, at its borders, contended for the land at the expense of weaker neighbours. Torn between Siena and Arezzo in a dispute that dragged on from the middle of the 7th century to the beginning of the 12th, it involved popes and emperors, concluding with the formal victory of the latter and the actual domination of the former. And it soon attracted the attention of the emerging city of Florence which saw it as a natural area for its own expansion.

The alleys of Volpaia are full of the atmosphere of another time.

After the conquest and destruction of Fiesole in 1125, Florence took over control of its territory which included the "historic" Chianti region with its border only a few miles from Siena. Conflict between the two cities was inevitable and hostilities began at the end of the century, often complicated by the claims of feudal lords who attempted to turn the situation to their own advantage. Although Florence's domination of Chianti (affirmed in an incontrovertible way with the Lodo di Poggibonsi of 1203) was challenged a number of times, Florentine supremacy became a reality through the establishment in the borderlands of a series of autonomous administrative jurisdictions, the "leagues". The one in Chianti was divided into three "terzieri" (thirds), corresponding more or less to the present towns of Radda, Castellina and Gaiole. But there was still to be no peace for this tormented borderland, which continued to feel the effects of any crisis that arose in the delicate political balance between the dominating cities up until the fall of the Sienese republic and its subsequent absorption into Medici territory.

From this time and up until the terrible summer of 1944, which left the area devastated after the wartime bombing, littered with mangled cannons and destroyed tanks, Chianti enjoyed a long period of peace, even if not yet one of prosperity.

... and the other on art

"In the year of Our Lord 1507 on the 29th of January, making a hole with an iron pole to plant vines, the pole broke into an ancient tomb of the Etruscans and there issued from the hole a fetid stench and they found

An unusual view of Chianti cloaked in a blanket of snow.

toward the road an exit leading out, closed with slabs of alberese stone and the room was cross shaped". This is the account, faithfully transcribed at the beginning of the 18th century by Filippo Buonarroti, a descendant of the great Michelangelo, of an eye-witness to the discovery. There follows the description of the funerary urns and of the rich objects in the tomb (8th-5th century BC), which is the very famous one of Montecalvario near Castellina.

One of the many tombs, all pillaged to a greater or lesser extent, which, together with the settlement discovered at Cetamura, near San Giusmè, are evidence of the important presence in Chianti of this people, in many ways still mysterious today, whose towns were strategically situated between Fiesole and Volterra. Apart from this, Antiquity seems to be represented here only by a protohistoric settlement (1st millenium BC) at Poggio la Croce near Radda, and by scattered finds of the Hellenistic (3rd-2nd century BC) and Roman periods.

However, despite the undoubted interest of these valuable finds, the Chianti that we know – with its ancient hamlets and farms, mills and ovens, country houses and villas, towers and castles, monasteries and abbeys, a few market towns and a scattering of little churches, oratories, chapels and mortuary tombs – was born in the Middle Ages.

To this difficult and fascinating age belongs the major part of the architectural patrimony of Chianti, whether concentrated in an ancient village, isolated on the top of a hill, overlooking a stream, or lost in a wood. Essential building, with structures almost always distinguished by a majestic simplicity and frequently in the Romanesque style, since the Gothic style, here, is an exception (San Pietro in Avenano).

Almost as if confirming its role as a borderland, Chianti is extremely rich in medieval fortifications: a line of south-facing Florentine castles (including

San Polo in Rosso, Lucignano, Brolio, Rencine and Montecastelli) corresponds on the opposite front to a line of Sienese castles (including Selvole, Cerreto, Riolo and Staggia); then further back are a myriad of fortified towns (Montefioralle, Volpaia, Radda, Vertine), many of which grew from ancient Roman settlements.

These were the so-called "walled lands": a ring of thick stone walls, punctuated by guard towers, defending dwellings, storehouses and stables that huddled around the lordly residence or "cassero", and the small main square with the church and the well. Unlike the religious buildings which, even when deconsecrated, have survived almost intact, there remains little today of the castles. Because even if they are still practically all within the area, often only the "cassero" remains, used as a rural dwelling, or otherwise they have been turned into villa-farms or country houses. In the worst cases only ruins remain, at times almost totally buried or hidden by vegetation.

Technology and art

Medieval workers constructed with taste and skill, favouring the use of local alberese stone with its different shades of colour ranging from ivory white to light gray, in blocks evenly squared and precisely assembled to form beautiful pointed arches. Their hand is recognizable in buildings of the 12th and 13th century while, contrary to what one might expect, from the 14th century the style seems to become coarser and even the material used, of poorer quality, was often obtained from the demolition of earlier buildings or consisted of rough-hewn quarry stones used with a great deal of mortar. Until in the 15th century the growing use of plaster permitted the concealment under a uniform and anonymous layer of a variety of different stone fragments and bricks

used in place of the beautifully chiseled stone that rarely survived in the archvaults, cornices and doorways.

The apse of the Romanesque church of San Donato in Poggio.

However much it remained on the periphery of the Renaissance and thus somewhat sheltered from the intense artistic and intellectual movement that developed elsewhere, Chianti was far from cut off: splendid evidence of this is the Commenda di Sant'Eufrosino at Volpaia. The Florentines, for their part, went to Chianti willingly to escape the humid heat of the city and purchased land, converting old feudal castles into "case da signore" – part villas and part agricultural concerns managed with entrepreneurial criteria. Land gave prestige, tranquillity and profit. And sharecropping was considered the ideal system. On the farm the "case da signore" and the "case da lavoratore" were made with the same materials and the same techniques: tiled roofs and brick floors, ceilings with beams, rafters and often whitewashed terracotta. Only the finishing touches were different: the richer houses had overhanging eaves, stone facing, stone frames around the doors and the windows with their wrought-iron gratings, an open loggia at the back opening onto a courtyard or garden; inside, vaulted or coffered ceilings and stone fireplaces.

In the fortifications of Castellina – and possibly elsewhere – the Medicean architect Giuliano da Sangallo (1445-1516) was involved. But besides forts and walls, evident traces of conflict between Florence and Siena abound in the late 16th century even in works that had little to do with war. Around this time two different urban models appear in the construction of noble buildings in Chianti: if on the one hand Baldassare Peruzzi (1431-1536) entered the scene with bricks, supported by the kilns active in

numerous locations, he was soon caught up by Bernardo Buontalenti (1536-1608) and pietra serena with its retinue of master stone-cutters.

"Chiantishire"

Many of these ancestral manors and elegant and serene villas today have become art centres, and sites for exhibitions, meetings, and shows; they have opened to agritourism and to the sale of farm products, or like the castle of Brolio, recast in full romanticism, constitute the splendid scenery of an imaginary and dreamy medieval age. And yet it was not too long ago that this secluded land,

The facade, redesigned by Benedetto Fortini (1919), of the stately Villa Vistarenni, built in the early 16th century by the Strozzi family.

excluded from the more frequented itineraries and great commercial roads, was unknown also to the many foreigners who between the 18th and 19th centuries made the Grand Tour in Italy the indispensable trip for those completing their intellectual education. At the time travel by stage-coach or in one's own carriage was possible only along the state roads, the only roads where one could be assured of postillions or at least a change of horses. And this excluded Chianti, where the only road worthy of the name was in a state of frightful degradation.

Until after the middle of the 19th century it was,

then, an unknown land, closed in its rusticity and reserved entirely for the sojourns, occasional and limited in time, of the few landed owners of the Florentine nobility for whom, besides a source of income, it was a place of relaxation and a rich hunting reserve. Here they could alternate pleasant leisure with the running of the agricultural concern, proceeding to embellish the landscape with villas, gardens and parks where, beginning in the 18th century, nature was "educated," corrected and civilized into "giardini della laetitia".

Then came the unexpected, sudden and constant wave of foreigners: fascinated visitors at first, then established residents, in that territory which because of the predominant presence of the English acquired a new suffix among the many that its name had enjoyed: it was ironically called "Chiantishire". And yet, the first to put down established roots was a Pole, Stanislao Poniatowski, who in 1810, following the secularization of ecclesiastical property ordered by the French government, received as a donation the Badia a Coltibuono, which his heirs were forced

Reproductions of old coats-of-arms at Gaiole in Chianti.

to sell after just twenty-five years. In the same way the Seduceschi family received the Badia a Passignano, sold by its descendants in the 1940s.

The experiment seemed to be over, except for the sporadic appearances – now in the 20th century – of international celebrities such as Bernard Berenson and Graham Greene who visited the writer Bino Samminiatelli at his country house at Vignamaggio.

In the meantime something was slowly but inexorably changing. While the road network was constantly being improved, new means of transportation were added to the old ones: first, the steam tramway that connected Florence to Greve and San Casciano, then later the automobile.

Already in the 27 September 1968 issue of the «New York Herald Tribune» one could read: "In Europe today a country house in Chianti converted into a holiday residence is very popular for a vacation: sophisticated English, Germans and Americans, and also a few Italians, have started to hunt for houses in the area that produces one of the most famous wines in Italy".

For the English, already traditionally tied to Florence, it was simply a matter of transferring their predilection to a new county, followed with great enthusiasm by the Dutch, Swiss, Americans and Germans. Some, after having found an ideal solution for vacations, took up permanent residence in the "rustici" abandoned by farmers in the 1950s, a choice that in many cases was accompanied by a direct and personal commitment to producing wine of high quality and developing receptive facilities in the area.

Black rooster on a gold field

They departed at the cock's crow on lightning chargers, the two champions. Racing at full gallop, they flew from Florence and from Siena one against the other as though in a tournament, because it had been decided that the territorial border between the two cities would be determined where the two would meet. The story teaches: when there is no solution one resorts to war, or to a contest. And a contest it was, won by the Florentines. With that genius that makes them special, they left their rooster unfed the night before, and he crowed very early the following morning, giving the starting signal to the rider. The Sienese rooster, well fed, woke later with his hymn to the rising sun, and the city champion left when his rival was already well on his way. Thus the border was fixed at Castellina, at a place later called Croce Fiorentina, a few miles from Siena.

The story, as we have seen, offers us a different version of the centuries-old conflict that from the first years of the 12th century until the middle of the 16th had seen the two cities opposed, each always straining to increase its territory at the expense of the other. So it is difficult to say whether it was the coat of arms of the League of Chianti proudly raised on its banner that generated *a posteriori* the legend of the contest, or

The “Gallo Nero” and “DOCG” on the neck of a typical “bordolese”.

The new agrarian landscape, with specialized plantations that have replaced the old mixed system.

whether on the contrary, this furnished Chianti with its symbol. However the facts occurred, we find our rooster next to the "ager Clanti et oppida eius", Chianti and its castles – Radda, Castellina and Brolio – which in 1547 Vasari painted in Florence in Palazzo Vecchio on the ceiling of the Salone dei Cinquecento. From here it scampered to the top of the tower of Castellina – which, even before Radda, was for a brief time the capital of the League – and then it leaped onto the coat of arms, raised in 1774, when Grand Duke Pietro Leopoldo replaced the old "terzieri" with the new Communities of Castellina in Chianti, Radda and Gaiole, an expression of local autonomy. In May

1924, when the "Consorzio per la difesa del vino tipico del Chianti e della sua marca d'origine" was founded in Radda – later to become the "Consorzio del Vino Chianti Classico" – it passed over to its flag, where it still extends its proud neck.

Stories...

If before the centralization of the grand dukes an anonymous chronicler could deplore the impossibility of "planting vines or harvesting grapes or even just living in peace on one's land," after the advent of the "Medicean Peace" in Tuscany the Florentines began to look upon the countryside as a source of investment and profit. In Chianti Michelangelo bought houses and fields and even chose a tower, around which in the last years of his life he built a "casa da oste". His letters often contained praises of the wine that he drank and offered his guests, especially that which he made personally, and which he even had sent as a gift to the pope. Machiavelli himself, embittered by the suspicion of his involvement in an anti-Medicean plot that continued to weigh on him even after his pardon, sought refuge (1512) in the poor lands he owned in Chianti. From the "Albergaccio" of Sant'Andrea in Percussina, where he worked on the draft of *The Prince* and perhaps even the *Florentine Histories*, the ex Secretary of the Florentine Republic loved to go to the inn to drink and play "a cricca, a triche-trach", before dressing again in "regal and courtly robes" and entering into communion with the great names of the past and the politics of the present.

Similarly, on his farm of Grignanello (Castellina in Chianti), the great Galileo Galilei (1564-1642) forgot his conflicts with official science and the accusations of heresy, taking pleasure "in the delicacy of the wines and the grapes and the ways of caring for the vines, which he himself with his own hands pruned

Galileo Galilei owned a farm at Castellina in Chianti.

and tied in the garden", as recalls his pupil Vincenzo Viviano who long preserved the memory of him and was buried with him. "Wine", wrote the scientist, "is like the blood of the land, the sun captured and transformed by such a complex structure as the grape berry, an admirable laboratory in which mechanisms, contrivances, processes and forces are coordinated by a hidden and perfect clinician. Wine is liquor of the utmost mastery, composed of humors and of light, by whose virtues the mind becomes luminous and clear, the soul expands, spirits are comforted and happiness is multiplied". The red wine of Chianti was the one he preferred and which he always took as a gift to his daughter, Sister Maria Celeste, and to her sisters.

Giuseppe Verdi (1813-1901) also enjoyed it, so much so that his wife, the famous singer Giuseppina Strepponi, wrote to a friend: "Verdi is very well, he eats, runs around the garden, sleeps and drinks Chianti, nothing but Chianti. Hurrah for Chianti and whoever found him such good wine".

We may also recall that in 1913, in the 17th-century villa of Count Chigi Saracini in the centre of Castelnuovo Berardenga, following an encounter with Arrigo Boito, the Accademia Chigiana was founded, which nineteen years later was moved to Siena. At Vignamaggio, instead, the famous Shakespearian actor and director Kenneth Branagh set his *Much Ado About Nothing* (1993).

... and tales

An oratory and a chapel near Panzano may well be the most ancient pieces of evidence of the cult attributed to saint Euphrosyne, the patron saint of Chianti. He is believed to have arrived here from his native Cappadocia in the final years of a long and tormented life dedicated to the active evangelization of this land and here, according to ancient tradition, he is said to be buried.

The buildings rise near a well of water that is claimed to be miraculous, and which in the 19th century attracted pilgrims from the furthest parts of Tuscany. As is often the case, this healing water is evidence of earlier pagan worship, a cult of extraordinarily long duration, however much Christianized in form. Some turn to it with eye disorders, though it is used mainly to increase the secretion of milk in breast-feeding mothers, and it is in this connection

Casks and grapes for Vinsanto.

of milk and water, both vital elements of life, that the cults honouring Mother Earth merge with ancient beliefs in the fertilizing power of life-creating water.

Alongside the great archetypal myths flourish a myriad of popular beliefs. Particularly strange is the following remedy for all kinds of ills: a pregnant woman slowly walks over the sick person lying on the ground, stepping on either side of the body and taking care not to touch the person with her feet. Two crossed irons, instead, ward off witches, while a shovelful of live embers outside the door protects against lightning.

If cures based on the infusion of rosemary against the loss of memory, olivewood against fears, egg whites for sprains and spiderwebs for wounds appear simple and naive to us, a certain perplexity is aroused over rubbing with stinging nettles to prevent or arrest hair loss, mouth rinses of horse urine to eliminate toothache, and the drinking of hot wine in which a little cow dung has been boiled to overcome melancholy.

There were other peasant remedies of not such remote times, like faith in the virtue of geraniums to keep away serpents, and the conviction that it was enough to see a robin redbreast fly high in the March sky to be immune from any illness for the whole year. A more poetic tradition was the ritual tying together of two bunches of broom by engaged couples on the mountain peak of San Michele as a token of their fidelity to each other. At one time this peak was called the "roof of Chianti" because from its summit, before reforestation, it was possible to take in the entire chain of the Chianti hills, the view reaching as far as the three main cities of Florence, Siena and Arezzo in the distance.

ZZANO
Verrazzano

Ancient spirits

The serenity of the landscape, the silence of the forest, the murmuring of the water, the paths of the faithful, the centres of intense religiosity should not however be misleading. Here also, auspicious beings and benevolent saints alternate with restless spirits and frightful apparitions. It is best not to alienate the ancient gods and to leave an offering to the god of forests Silvanus and to the god of agriculture Palus, *Pales* in Latin, accompanying it perhaps with a propitiatory chant. But above all is the need to placate Aplu, Apollo of the silver bow; if invoked ritually, during the day he will be benevolent to hunters, drawing animals near with his music and sending their shots to the mark, while at night he will not hesitate to torment them capriciously, ripping off their blankets and – a demonic nightmare – crouching down on their chests.

More recent but no less fearful is the malevolent presence of the soul of Bettino Ricasoli (1809-1880), the "Iron Baron", so called not only for his rigid character but also for the harsh control he exercised over his farmers and the inflexibility with which he tyrannized his family. In this way he was able to rebuild his family fortunes and reach the highest levels in politics. Governor of Tuscany on behalf of Vittorio Emanuele II in 1859, he prepared its annexation to Piedmont; later, he was twice prime minister of the newborn Kingdom of Italy. His successes in agriculture, business and politics, however, were

Fierce political satire directed at Bettino Ricasoli, suspected of rigging elections and referendums.

not enough to save his immortal soul from the "black legend". Tradition has it that during his funeral ceremony in the chapel of the family's ancestral castle at Brolio, a powerful gust of wind blew open doors and windows and dashed the four candles of the catafalque to the floor, extinguishing them immediately. Interesting the similarity between this frightful event and the medieval ritual of excommunication, which called for the overturning of the candles and violently extinguishing them on the floor to signify the loss of divine light and the condemnation of sin to darkness. It almost seems that the powers of the afterlife had wanted to confirm the excommunication effectively inflicted on the baron for his contribution to the suppression of several religious orders and the confiscation of numerous ecclesiastical properties. However it was, from then on his ghost began to appear, on foot or on horseback, on the neo-Gothic bastions and along the paths of the park, flinging open, banging, breaking and smashing. To exorcise the diabolical presence a Capuchin friar was summoned, who conducted a second funeral ceremony. As the coffin carried on shoulders grew heavier and heavier, the elements broke into a rage a second time and were placated only when the damned soul of the great baron was chained by a powerful exorcism in the denseness of the thicket by one of the streams descending from the hills to the east of the castle. Even if now his body rests in the chapel, it is there that he continues to appear with frightful howls, the galloping of horses and the clattering of wheels.

But Ricasoli was not the only damned soul: his diabolical companions were Batano (possibly the farmer, his accomplice in the looting of the Church) and the priest Manescalchi, guilty of having made him invulnerable with a blasphemous ceremony of the consecration of the host in the palm of his hand.

Divine pleasure

By whatever name he was invoked, in various ages and at different latitudes, Dionysus, Fufluns, Libero, Bacchus, the inebriating and inebriated god, joyful and dancing, lord of the unbridled senses, of a wild life and of passionate love, he found the land of his choosing in the Tuscan hills.

Fossils of *Vitis vinifera*, dating back millions of years, found in the travertine in the land around San Vivaldo, tell us that Tuscany has always been a land of wine. But even without going back so far in time, if it is true that this land entered history with the Etr-

Malvasia del Chianti. From 2005 allowed only in the grapes used to make Vinsanto.

uscans (8th-7th century BC), then wine entered it with them. The type of wine produced then is unknown.

If the peoples who after the fall of the Roman Empire went up and down the peninsula plundering and overthrowing civil order and turning much of the Italian countryside into wasteland, in this secluded area, far from communication routes, monks – especially Benedictines and Vallombrosans – soon began to preserve and transcribe ancient documents linked to agronomy and viticulture and to put their rules into practice. Monks of solitary places and forested zones, they not only provided assistance to the poor and wayfarers in mountain areas scoured by bands of brigands and criminals, but they also tended woods and meadows and cultivated fields often dotted with

Wine-drinking during a medieval feast.

olive trees and vines. Thus, although the legend attributing to them the introduction of vine cultivation to Chianti may not be true, we must attribute its expansion to these Orders, beginning with abbeys like Coltibuono and Passignano.

Both on their own lands, and on those of the secular clergy, laymen and, from the year 1000, the bourgeoisie, the "specialized" cultivation of the vine increased, grown low to the ground in rows, often protected – almost a sacred space – in closed gardens or in cloistered areas, or even by city walls to protect them from robbery and damage caused by livestock. Via della Vigna Vecchia and Via della Vigna Nuova, Via Vinegia, Santa Maria in Vigna (later Santa Maria Novella) in Florence, testify to the planting of vines at the edges of, or inside, the city. Unauthorized persons were prohibited from entering the vineyards; damage caused by them or by livestock was severely punished; their destruction could even lead to torture of the suspect. Conversely, a heavy tax was imposed on wine and quality had to be paid for on the basis of the valuations of the Catasto (land registry office).

In taberna quando sumus...

In 913 the first parchment documents containing a clear reference to wine-making in Chianti were discovered in the church of Santa Cristina at Lucignano. A long silence follows until, at the beginning of the millennium, they seem to become more frequent.

Thus, in February of 1023 "at Grignano, in the jurisdiction of Florence", we have information about the concession of "arable and vineyard" land to a tenant farmer who undertakes to improve it, and we know that at more or less the same time the lords of Brolio, the Ricasoli, planted vines on the steep and rocky slopes dominated by their castle.

The revival was favored by the rise of the cities which saw in the commerce of wine an important source of wealth. An indication of this, in Florence, was the foundation in the second half of the 13th century of the Wine Merchants' Guild, the most important of the Lesser Guilds, together with the opening of new inns and wine cellars. If the bells of the *Angelus* signaled the closure of the city gates at sundown, the *bibitorum* of the drinkers forced the closure of the wine shops: the transition from a luxury commodity to a popular and general one had by now occurred.

A sign of joy and of wealth, of excess and of transgression, wine was present at every table to "correct" the often unhealthy water, just as this, in turn, reduced the danger of intoxication. It was, moreover, considered a real food, and as such was used to succour the poor, the weak and the ill. Also, for lack of anything better, even weak "acquarello", the light wine obtained from the second and third pressings, appeared in the diets of both city and country workers as a vital supplement to a diet that was often insufficient and lacking in energy.

We can also assume that it was regarded as appropriate for various other uses, if in 1213 the ecclesiastical authorities were compelled to ban baptisms administered with wine or oil.

White wine, red wine

However much it was subjected to ever higher taxes and thus to continual price rises, wine was consumed in considerable quantities. Tuscan wine was called “rutilante”, or “vermiglio”, or if white, “vernaccia”. The name “Chianti” appeared late in medieval documents, and when we finally find it in a business contract signed in 1398 with which Ser Lapo Mazzei (1350-1412), man of letters, jurist, and economist in the Florentine government, authorizes the payment of “6 casks... of wine”, we discover immediately that it is the “white wine of Chianti”, a product then quite different from that which would later be introduced to the world.

In the same collection of letters we also find the mention of wines – this time red – "di Valdigrieve" by Amedeo Gherardini, a friend of Francesco Datini who often took care of their affairs and he mentions in particular a wine from Uzzano and another that had been "put into casks at Vignamag(i)o", both from land he owned between Montefioralle and Panzano. Wines, however, that the Catasto in Florence in 1427 distinguished strictly from those of "Chianti with all its province" – whose territory did not comprise the northern zones, those that are included in the present district of Greve – which were judged to be decidedly superior.

Precisely when Chianti finally became red we do not know: no more, at least, than

The elliptical structure of Montefioralle, with its turreted walls, developed with ring-roads and radial alleys around the 12th-century "cassero".

we can know the organic composition of the grapes of that time, the alcoholic content, the sugar level, the taste or aroma of the wine. They are lost forever, among the fragments of a past that are impossible to restore, to taste, to recognize. Documentary sources found in archives or gleaned from literature help us little, so vague and uncertain are the notations.

Only in the 17th century would the verses of the Ferrarese poet Fulvio Testi send us a more explicit message: "But if you come, I, of the Etruscan Chianti / equal to rubies I will pour out dew for you / that kisses you and bites you and makes / sweet tears stream from your eyes".

Blood of Chianti

Even before it was called "Chianti" the red wine produced in the zone was famous for the freshness and brilliance conferred on it by the "governo", the exclusive process of wine-making that had been written about as long ago as 1364 by two Florentines, Giovanni di Durante and Ruberto di Guido Bernardi, a goldsmith. This process consisted of adding a small percentage of dried grapes to wine just drawn from the vat and letting it referment to obtain a product that was free of impurities, clear and full-bodied. While Giovanni recommended black grapes, Ruberto prescribed white grapes pressed and allowed to ferment, suggesting that it was a good idea not to contaminate the vats by washing them with water, but to leave a little wine from the previous year to "keep guard". Both, in accordance with the tastes of the time, suggested egg whites, bitter almonds and salt to clarify it, and pepper and rose petals to give it colour.

Chianti, then, was famous among Tuscan wines, but was not the best. This can be inferred from the valuation registered in the above-mentioned Florentine Catasto of 1427: the quite respectable figure of 36 soldi a barrel fixed for the "vermigli" of very small

Traditional cart with demijohns.

highly regarded areas, was in fact surpassed by that established for the whites of some localities of the upper Valdarno.

"The Chianti valley produces excellent wine", declared the humanist Cristoforo Landino in 1481, and over a hundred years later, in 1596, Andrea Bacci, a physician at the papal court of Sixtus V, placed it first among the Tuscan wines. Another hundred years on, in the *Ditirambo di Bacco e Arianna* the chief physician at the court of the Tuscan Grand Dukes, Francesco Redi (1626-1698), a remarkable "man of letters and science", although giving the prize to the wine of Montepulciano as "the king of all wines", sang praises to the same god in the famous eulogy: "My tongue already astute / tastes a little, savors this other / robust wine that boasts / of being born in the heart of Chianti [...] Majestic / Imperious / it walks within my heart / and silently chases away / every worry and every pain".

Wine of the law

Excellent for exorcizing anxieties and pains of the soul, but equally effective against bodily ills, insisted Redi in *Arianna inferma* with these less well-known verses: "And that which matters, the physician, / and in one hundred thousand cases, / has again given proof of its virtue / celebrating it more than just wine of Chianti". Divine nectar, then, heavenly and miraculous beverage, as the timeless and amusing *Litanie del vino* confirm, assuring that "And the Eternal Father said / he who does not drink goes to hell", since, as everyone should know and bear well in mind, "All the angels and saints drink only Chianti wine".

A wine to guard then, to protect, to defend its good name and quality. Fairly early on, the Chianti League had dealt with this problem, issuing a decree in 1444 which expressly prohibited the harvesting of grapes before the feast of Saint Michael, which was in late September, "because wine cannot be good and afterwards could not be sold". But the time also arrived when it was necessary to impose penalties of various degrees and types for those who cut or in some way adulterated the original product. In the early 17th century the alteration of the seals fixed to the containers called for "two lashes to be administered in the Old Market with the words around one's neck saying: falsifier of flasks".

Yet in spite of measures issued at various times, it wasn't until 1716 that the Bando of Grand Duke Cosimo III, anticipating modern legislation, tackled the problem in a comprehensive way, taking care not only to establish the terms of production and sale of some of the most famous Tuscan wines, but to protect their denomination by establishing the borders of the various zones and levying heavy penalties for cases of clandestine trafficking and imitation.

A decisive step forward in production technique

took place thanks to the works of Cosimo Trinci (1738), and above all to the studies on wine-making by Giovanni Cosimo Villifranchi, who considered "Chianti" to be among the best Tuscan wines. It is to the latter we are indebted for useful information, for in his *Oenologia toscana* (1773) he informs us of how "Chianti, Pomino and Artimino" are "wines that last a long time and rarely suffer during long trips [...] the simplest in composition and the least complex for the type of grape that contribute to give

them substance and that spirit they have [...] a large part of the black Canaiolo and a somewhat lesser quantity of S. Gioveto, Mammolo and Marzamino". For the "governo", instead, the must of the "Colore dolce" was used, that in the years in which the wine is too sharp or the colour too intense, was replaced with white Canaiolo or with Trebbiano. Thus a wine "of a very full ruby colour" was produced, which, given the considerable demand in Italy and abroad, early on began to suffer since "many producers, eager to profit and unwilling to decline requests, cut Chianti wine with wine from other places", such that it was necessary to make the wise decision to no longer ship it in casks, but rather in flasks". It must have been a widespread habit, difficult to break and impossible to suppress, if in that same year the new

Grand Duke Pietro Leopoldo, in the course of a visit to Chianti, observed that "the best places for wine are Brolio and Ama. The small producers adulterate it and thus discredit it: the good large producers do not do this and earn what they want, making it of top quality and with much care since it is very highly regarded, especially in England".

Wine of the past

If the composition of the land and its position, the choice of grapes and the custom of keeping the vines low were good requirements for a high quality wine, it seems that the process of wine-making in Chianti differed little from the traditional method adopted in the rest of Tuscany until the first half of the last century.

Just before the harvest, which normally took place at the beginning of October, certain qualities of grapes were selected that were brought into the houses in large baskets and spread out to dry out on rush matting, wicker mats and racks. The other grapes were packed into wooden tubs and loaded onto carts to be taken into the vat rooms and

The press for manual grape-crushing.

poured into the large chestnut vats with beechwood hoops, usually with open tops. This was the place where the must was made, crushing by foot or with a board attached to a long pole the cake of skin and stems that rose to the surface during the process of fermentation. This was repeated many times during the day until the lowering of the level of pulp indicated that the process had ended. At this point the separation began, and, having once poured off the choice wine ("vino fiore"), the pomace was put through the wine press many times to increase, albeit to the detriment of the quality, the quantity of the "vino stretto" destined for family use.

The old practice of "governo", also known as "all'uso toscano", a usage that makes the wine of these areas so special, giving aroma and fragrance, was adopted throughout the entire region. As an alternative to the usual system, about which we have already spoken, one could carry out the "governo a mosto", so called because instead of adding grapes that had been selected and dried on rush mats to the vats, they went to the wine press and the must was added directly to the casks. If a second "governo", or "rigoverno", took place in the spring, Colorino grapes were preferred due to their conservability. Either with the maceration of the pulp together with the stems, usually carried out in open vats and with periodic pressing, typical of the first method, or with the operation of delayed separation and correction after casking typical of the second method, the result was always the characteristic "frizzante" and early maturation of Tuscan wines, even those of high prestige, which made them so pleasant to taste yet so unsuitable for ageing.

These practices probably gave rise to the local

production of Vinsanto, which today mixes the white grapes of Trebbiano and Malvasia, dried and made into wine between November and February, to which a small amount of Zibibbo grapes was once added. The must, obtained after having selected the grapes, separated them from the stems, from the skins, and from the seeds, was aged for four years in small barrels in spacious lofts and served to guests and friends. It is rare and precious, then, whether "dolce" or "amabile", or – as preferred today – dry like an aristocratic sherry.

Wine in the Academy

Pietro Leopoldo (1747-1792) had a dream when, barely eighteen, he was appointed by the imperial family – the Hapsburgs – to the grand-ducal throne of Tuscany: to revitalize a ruined economy with a policy independent of Vienna and the support of valid collaborators. His reform programme was directed primarily toward the precarious and neglected world of agriculture. Here he moved in two directions: aiding small property owners and developing the Accademia dei Georgofili (Agricultural Academy), the oldest in the agrarian field in Europe (1753). On their model farm near Bagno a Ripoli – where the road that leads from Florence to Chianti begins – the Georgofili began an intense activity, awarding prizes of money for new initiatives, putting into practice the traditional mixed cultivation of vines, olive trees, mul-

Portrait of the young grand-duke Pietro Leopoldo.

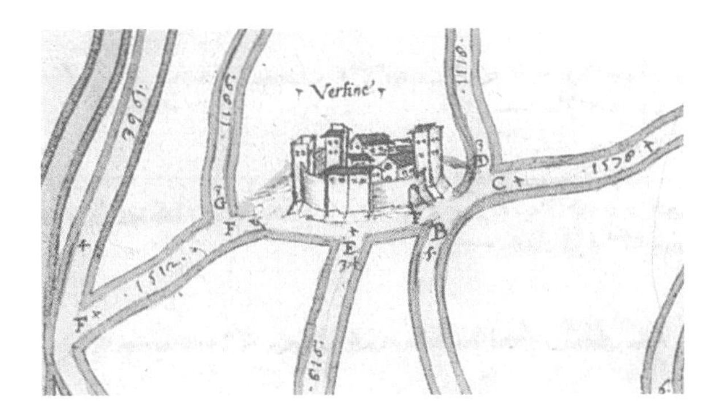

Vertine in the Map of the Capitani di Parte Guelfa.

berry trees and fruit trees in fields of grain and teaching about innovative and revolutionary crops such as tobacco.

They had also experimented successfully with new combinations of grapes, creating an excellent wine with the reds of Sangiovese and Canaiolo and the whites of Trebbiano and Malvasia; a product that was unsuccessful, however, because of its poor inclination for ageing and due to the irresistible rise of the more pleasant Bordeaux and the more refined Burgundy. They tried various formulas, mixing Canaiolo, Sangiovese and Mammolo in equal parts to obtain a wine that would age, a robust wine with an intense colour; and to Canaiolo and to Mammolo they added Trebbiano and Occhio di Pernice in equal parts, giving them a wine that was lighter in colour and more delicate to the taste.

But in spite of everything, farmers knew very little about how to make wine; they amassed ripe and unripe grapes, healthy and mouldy ones together in wooden tubs; they knew nothing about the point of equilibrium between acidity and sugar level; they farmed well but made wine badly. And the landed aristocracy, the holders of power and money, were for the most part absentees and little interested in investing in the land.

Wine at the castle

The Iron Baron, instead, loved the mean, rocky land on which he intended to live for not only the brief harvest period or the hunting season. And he wanted it fertile, prosperous and properly cultivated by industrious, God-fearing hands. A rather strange character, Bettino Ricasoli, anchored to the past in the paternalistic management of the farm, though an innovator in his ready adoption of English-style crop rotation, in the boost he gave to livestock rearing, in the establishment of a proper code for "Chianti", a wine that in the formula transcribed in the letter he sent to Professor Studiati in Pisa in 1880, "receives from Sangioveto the principal amount of its aroma [...] and a certain robustness; from Canajolo the pleasantness which tempers the harshness of the former, without taking away any of the fragrance which it has as well; Malvagia, which wines destined for ageing could well do without, tends to dilute the product of the first two grapes, it increases its flavour and renders it lighter and more readily usable at the daily table". Along with a more precise proportion of grapes, whose composition he had disclosed some years earlier (70% Sangiovese, 15% Canaiolo and an equal amount of Malvasia for wines produced for immediate consumption; the abolition of Malvasia and a higher percentage of Sangiovese for wines made for ageing), he imposed stricter controls over the wine-making process, ordering the separation of the pulp from the stems, the use of closed containers for fermentation and a rapid transfer of wine from the vats, followed by the "governo all'uso toscano" for the fresh and effervescent "rosso beverino". And these operations he also describes in detail in a letter: "Every effort is made to fill the vats in 24 hours. Fermentation is begun

The old system of upper ventilation, functioning perfectly, in the cellars of Badia a Passignano.

at this time. At the end of six days it has been completed... and then the wine is drawn from the vats. Once the wine has been collected, which flows naturally from the tap, the pulp is pressed, and the wine that emerges is added to the former in casks, in which fermentation continues".

In 1878 the "new formula Chianti" triumphed at the Paris Exhibition, although even in 1876 the oenologist Giuseppe Frojo could write that "Tuscany is the region of Chianti, whose fame is ancient and still justified. It is of a lively but not intense colour, has a delicate aroma, a right amount of alcohol; it is always fresh and smooth, moreover it is quickly digested; it is therefore a wine second to none [...] when treated well it can be stored and also keeps well when transported by sea. Such an example is provided by the Chianti of Brolio, which owes its perfection to the assiduous care of Baron Bettino Ricasoli, and which in England now costs dearly". Thus were confirmed the predictions of Repetti, who already in 1833 had written that "the ever increasing fields, due to the intelligent attention of the present Baron, have converted the woody slopes of Brolio into a picturesque amphitheater for the variety, abundance and goodness of its products, among which for their excellence are the famous wines".

Wine of the present

The foundations of "Chianti" had by now been laid, and it is worth stating again that the original formula excluded the use of Malvasia for wines destined for ageing, while Trebbiano, of which excessive use would later be made, was not named at all. Thus, the recent tendency to limit the use of white grapes, with the idea of avoiding them entirely, merely confirms the preferences of the Baron. And yet, wine made from different kinds of grapes has

not remained constant because the proportions have been modified not only in the course of time but also in relation to the distribution of cultivations of vine plants on the various farms, with a progressive reduction of secondary ones, and a marked tendency to increase Sangiovese. A process, this, which has been far from peaceful, on the contrary it has been stormy and full of unexpected developments.

It began with oidium – the white mildew which from 1845 destroyed three quarters of Tuscan grape production – followed shortly after by phylloxera, an insect which, introduced with plants imported to France from Colorado, irreparably ruined most of the European vines. The solution was a drastic one: local vines were grafted onto the rootstocks of American vines which by this time were immune due to their long exposure to the parasite. Once these scourges had been overcome, there remained another, in many respects equally serious problem, that of the recurrent arrival on the market of large quantities of poor-quality wine that undermined the prestige of the genuine product. Once producers had found a valid system of defense by producing a distinguishing label for authentic "Chianti", three problems still remained: establishing the territorial limits of the production, preventing abuses and protecting the wine from deterioration caused by transportation. While the former turned out to be the thorniest – such that even today the confines of this small area of land are the subject of violent controversies typified by the now celebrated slogan: "There's no Chianti outside Chianti" – the others were promptly confronted with diligence and resolve.

Chianti protects itself...

It was not that long ago when only the large companies could sell their product directly, while small farmers were forced to depend on intermediaries, to whom they sold their entire lot in advance. In fact, the only restriction imposed by the law regarded the date of the wine's introduction on the market: the February following the harvest for "mezzo Chianti", and not before June for quality "Chianti". Thus, the very moment it emerged from the cellars – either in barrels or in the characteristic straw-covered flasks protected by a layer of oil and by a little paper "hat" – wine escaped completely from any control and could with impunity be adulterated either with other inferior wines or with wines of a different origin, or even be sold with a different label.

In 1860 Adolfo Laborel Melini, of the family of wine-producers from Pontassieve, had given the problem an early solution, creating, with the help of the local De Grollé glassworks, a "tempered" or "strapeso" flask able to withstand corking with a cork stopper under pressure. There were many obvious advantages to this. A wine thus packaged was not only protected from abuses, but was also not subject to loss during transport and the consumer ran no risk – more common than one might imagine – of drinking an unpleasant mixture of wine and oil. The only inconvenience was the higher cost of the flask, which as a result was used only for superior

Wine flasks with their traditional reed-plaited covering.

products and for shipments abroad via rail. Humble table wine continued for a long time to travel with its little paper hat.

The problem of authenticity returned cyclically in the 1960s, but this time it was made worse by the flight of farmers from the countryside and by the decline of production based on obsolete techniques of wine-making, with high costs and modest profits. In actual fact too much was badly produced, with unselected genetic material of low quality, grafting rootstocks that were too robust, and an excessive spacing of the rows; and if traditional labour could no longer be relied upon, changes imposed by mechanization invariably proved to be excessively burdensome. As white wine made from Trebbiano –

which was neither selected nor made into wine professionally – was rejected by the market, its grapes – with the authorization of a codified regulation that tolerated up to 25-30% of it – were added to the already high percentage of Canaiolo to impoverish the composition of a "Chianti" that was no longer "Chianti". Diluted, brick-coloured, sharp, tannic, devoid of body and roundness and lacking any aroma, it was just about unsellable. In the end fate would decide that a case of flagrant adulteration – circulated by the Italian and international press, with consequent measures taken by the government aimed at eliminating abuses and subsidies from the European Economic Community for the planting of new vines – signalled the start of a revival of a wine that had become altered and devalued, causing wine production to be viewed from a new perspective, that of rationalization in the name of profit, though above all of quality.

Woods and vineyards - the two most typical expressions of the Chianti region today.

... and defends itself

Slowly, the most urgent problem also came to be solved: the territorial definition of the Chianti area. The question could be considered solvable from a historical point of view, since on the first map of Tuscany drawn up by Girolamo Bellarmati in 1536, the territory coinciding with the "terzieri" of the ancient League was indicated by this name. But by the beginning of the 19th century, perhaps contemporaneously with the partial transformation, in a capitalistic sense, of the agrarian structure and with the growing prestige of its wine on the markets, the name had gradually come to include the valleys of the Pesa and the Arbia and almost all the Val di Greve, whose environmental characteristics at that time appeared not too dissimilar from those of the historic Chianti area and which produced an equally prestigious wine. The confusion increases if the region is examined from a purely geographical viewpoint. The only obvious reference is in fact the crest of the Monti del Chianti, which marks the border with the upper Valdarno. We can see, then, that it is a nebulous territorial entity which has always been forced into the confines of an artificial boundary. If we then add that Chianti was situated at the meeting-point of the medieval dioceses of Arezzo, Siena and Volterra (the latter substituted in the 16th century by Colle Valdelsa), Fiesole and Florence, for centuries involved in a battle for scraps of land, we can only conclude that there exists not one Chianti, but many: the classic, the historical, the ecclesiastical, the geographical, the political, the oenological, the Chianti of the League. And, above all, there exist both a real Chianti and an imaginary one.

The permanent consolidation of the various territories, all physically and historically diverse, was therefore an extremely laborious operation, which proved to be feasible only by virtue of their common oenological vocation. The Sindacato Enologico Chiantigiano was founded in 1903 with the aim of ensuring that the name "Chianti" be used only for wine coming from the zone typical of the production, which included all the hill territory between Florence and Siena along with the valleys of the Greve and Pesa, and anticipated the possibility of a later extension to "outlying places". The king's government reacted slowly, granting in 1911 the right to add the specification "in Chianti" only to the towns of the League, and in 1924 passing a law that controlled the wine sector.

Immediately, at Radda, a group of producers in the zone created the Consorzio per la Difesa del Vino Tipico del Chianti e della sua Marca d'Origine – the present Consorzio del Vino Chianti Classico, then called "Gallo nero" because they were the holders of the ancient coat of arms of the League – that was dedicated to defining the area of production. Three years later, the vine-growers of Rufina, Montalbano and the hills to the north of Florence would create the Consorzio del Vino Chianti Putto which, under the symbol of a florid cherub on a blue background (which with slight modifications was inspired by the one executed by Verrocchio for the first Courtyard of Palazzo Vecchio), comprised most of the Florentine vineyards excluded from the Classico.

Chianti today

Official recognition was ratified by a law of 1932 which, citing as justification its substantial geo-pedological, morphological and climatic homogeneity, which are those factors that determine in the most direct way the particular attributes of the wine, included in the territory of production all of central Tuscany with various additional areas that stretched almost as far as the coast. In this area, divided into seven sub-zones – "the Chianti area of Classico,

Colour: a vivid ruby-red, turning to garnet with ageing.

Montalbano, Rufina, Colli Fiorentini, Colli Aretini, and Colline Pisane e Senesi" – wine had to be produced with the "traditional" Chianti vine plants (Sangiovese, Canaiolo, Malvasia and... Trebbiano!) – and be of a consistent quality.

The borders of the various areas, made official in 1955 on the map of the Istituto Geografico Militare di Firenze, were reaffirmed in 1967 by a law that brought about a revolution in the economic-productive and territorial order with the creation of thousands of hectares of specialized vineyards. This law regulated the varieties of vines that could be planted, and fixed a maximum hectare yield limit with the clear intent of favouring quality as opposed to quantity. Correction was allowed with wine, must or grapes from other sources, and the alcohol content and ageing necessary to obtain the qualification of "Vecchio" or "Riserva" for the wines of the various zones was established. On this basis a denominazione di origine controllata (DOC) was defined that extended to other territories of ancient wine-making tradition – Montespertoli, Cerreto Guidi, Gambassi, Agliana and San Miniato – areas which were not allowed, however, to add the indication of provenance of their "Chianti". Even in 1984, the first draft of the production regulations for the DOCG (denominazione di origine controllata e garantita) of Chianti and Chianti Classico, although imposing on "Classico" stricter rules than those anticipated for the other "Chianti", considered it a sub-denomination of a single DOCG. Problems of another kind were to follow. In 1992 the use, in any language other than Italian, of the words "Gallo Nero" was prohibited on any informational or advertizing material. In the interests of retaining this saying even abroad, it was left untranslated and so became a kind of universal slogan. With a sensational verdict the exclusive right to

Vines with the Monti del Chianti behind.

use it was granted only to the American wine producers "Gallo Winery" of Ernest and Julio Gallo who had claimed it as their own. Only in 1996 did the Ministerial Decree of August 5th recognize DOCG Chianti Classico as an independent denomination, thus clearly and definitively admitting its diversity and peculiarity compared to other wines.

Classifying "Chianti"

We are talking about an extensive production area, with different types of terrain, microclimates that vary every few hundred meters, differing alignments of vines, farming practices tied to local traditions (although by now surpassed by a common technology) and wine made from different grapes with percentages varying according to the sub-zones. It is illuminating, in this context, to read about the various measures that over time have regulated the types of vines to be planted in a modern Chianti vineyard, in which the progressive reduction of white grapes and Canaiolo and the disappearance of Colorino have seen in turn the introduction of a small percentage of "black grapes coming from vines recommended and/or authorized in the administrative units of the production area of the grapes", units precisely listed in the most recent "disciplinare di produzione" (Decree of August 5, 1996; Decree of May 16, 2002). It is natural therefore that alongside robust and full-bodied wines, richer in tannin and suitable for long ageing, wines are produced with a lower alcohol content but more fragrance, suitable for medium ageing, and others still that are for more immediate consumption. If we add to all this the existence, in each of these areas, of companies that are able to produce wines with diverse characteristics, we can justifiably assert that there hardly exists a zone in which the "damned Tuscans" don't produce their "Chianti".

The radical break with the past has taken place over the last twenty years, with the rediscovery of the potential of Sangiovese – especially if it comes from vineyards of low yield and is used on its own to make wine – and the production of wines made with non-native grapes. Full-bodied wines, noble and refined, but nevertheless "non-Chianti in Chianti".

There are stricter regulations for "Chianti Classico", now very different from those of the Iron Baron. Not only has the maximum production of the vineyards been almost halved compared to previous norms, but the adoption of precise planting schemes is required, forms of vine cultivation and pruning systems that do nothing to modify the particular characteristics of the grapes and of the wine, the prohibition of any form of training over a horizontal roof or any forcing practice. There is also careful selection of appropriate vine plants identified as those whose soils, at an altitude not higher than 700 metres above sea level, "are constituted prevalent-

ly by arenaceous, marly-calcareous substrata, by argillaceous schist, by sand and stones" with a maximum production of grapes of 75 quintals per hectare.

And that is not all. Allowing white grapes (Trebbiano and Malvasia) up to a maximum of 6% (though only up to the grape-harvest of 2005 inclusive) and relegating autochthonous black grapes (Canaiolo and Colorino) or "international" black grapes (Cabernet Sauvignon and Merlot) to a secondary role (20%), the aim is for the predominance of a Sangiovese of superior quality, whose minimum percentage is fixed at 80% but which can also be used to make wine on its own (100%). The minimum alcohol content is high (12°) and the ageing period is long (this quality wine can be sold only from October 1 of the year following the harvest. The minimum alcohol content required for "Chianti Classico" Riserva is even higher (12.5°) and for this wine at least twenty-four months ageing is necessary, of which at least three in the bottle.

San Leonino
at Panzano in Chianti.

Grapes and surroundings

This land has never produced wine only. At one time, instead of the large expanses of specialized vineyards, one could see vines growing together with olive trees and tracts of wheat ripening in the midst of them: vestiges of an ancient world, where the land of each farm had to be used for a multitude of family needs.

It may be that the sharp and slightly bitter oil of Chianti's small green olives was once prized by the Romans, who used it not only as a condiment but also for illumination, for softening women's skin and for massaging the muscles of athletes.

The countryside yielded cereal grains, fruit and vegetables, while the woods were an incomparable reserve for man and beast. Not only did they sup-

Oil-jars and a moment of the oil-harvest. Chianti Classico olive oil has a centuries-old tradition.

ply firewood and timber for construction and fresh meat to alternate with that of courtyard animals, but they were also exploited for pasturage and forage; the grass of the undergrowth, the foliage of shrubs, and a plentiful supply of acorns that covered the ground between October and January.

Used until relatively recent times even in the human diet, acorns were preserved in large baskets or lightly toasted in the ovens in which bread was baked to avoid fermentation and then ground for the preparation of mash. Forests also provided straw for the stalls, herbaceous plants and berries for consumption.

Thus, as early as 1773, in the course of his visit

to Chianti, Pietro Leopoldo could note that it was "full of small landowners, neither rich nor poor", who "live on grain, wine and silk... and on acorns for the many pigs; there is also oil and many chestnut trees in the mountains with grazing areas in the forests for cattle and sheep, especially in spring and summer" and that the farmers were well kept, "farming being very laborious."

If in the past ten years the slopes of the Chianti hills have been levelled as a result of bulldozing to create terrain for the new vineyards that now are everywhere, changing the face of this land more than any of the turbulent events of the past had ever done, there was a time when an inimitable balance had been created between productive activity, forms of settlement and the rural landscape.

On the other hand, the mixed system was also responsible for the low productive yield of the land: too many plants disturbed each other, since the working of a piece of land is done according to what is cultivated on it, and it may be that what is needed to grow grains can at the same time damage the vines. Clayey soil, for example, needs deep plowing, because where water stagnates roots that have risen to the surface in search of air suffer damage as a result of drought: olives fall, grapes fail to ripen.

It is just as well, therefore, that the dry period comes in September, because in July or August an excessively dry climate would alter the synthesis of sugars, negatively influencing the strength of the wine. Types of fertilizer, methods of pruning and the cultivation itself of the plants vary from plot to plot and closely respond to the type of fruit that is grown. Even fertility is a relative concept. For the vine, for example, the aim is not so much to produce a great quantity, but to produce grapes of a high quality. Just like aromatic plants that thrive in dry, rocky soils, the more it grows in soil lacking

nutrients, the more it develops aroma and fragrance. This is why the soil of Chianti is suitable for the vine.

A "casa colonica" (farmhouse) "in continual expansion", with additional buildings arranged picturesquely next to the original turreted nucleus.

Life on the farm

Life in Chianti cannot have changed much over the centuries, at least not until very recent times, times marked by changes that have profoundly affected all aspects of it – methods of working, customs, ways of life, the inhabitants themselves.

Each farm was self-sufficient. And working the land was not the only hard and laborious process. Water had to be drawn from the fountain and women carried it in pitchers, balancing the jars on their heads on small cushions improvised from rags. Everyone baked bread in their own oven, crushed olives in their own oil mill and pressed grapes in their

own wine press. Chickens and rabbits were raised for meat, but also for eggs and pelts: in the stables there were sheep and pigs, and occasionally a pair of oxen. Farmers sowed, reaped, threshed, returned mineral salts to the earth with the plowing in of fava beans, and harvested their own olives. At the end of autumn chestnuts and mushrooms were gathered in the woods, and between January and February a pig was slaughtered. And there were the animals to yoke to the plow or the cart for harvesting. Baskets were woven and wooden tubs were made for the grape harvest, casks and barrels for the making of wine, mats for drying the bunches of grapes; flasks and demijohns were covered with straw, animals were tended, sheep were washed and shorn, horses shod, tools

The pleasantly old-fashioned interior of the master's house.

forged, farm buildings were constructed – vat room, cellar, oil mill, stable, pigsty, sheep pen, fertilizer pit, stores for fodder – and even houses.

Rosary beads were carved from the hard bulbs of irises, as were "dentaroli" for massaging the gums of breast-feeding babies. At times, simple wooden or wicker sledges could take the place of the cart, and even prove to be more useful in hilly zones that were unreachable by road. The only really vital external presence was that of the farrier to shoe the animals and the blacksmith to sharpen blades, or that of the peddler to replace some item of prime necessity. The city was far away, there was little familiarity with the veterinarian, with the doctor even less, and often a handful of herbs had a better effect on man and beast than any medical prescription.

It was a whole mental universe connected to conditions of life that were profoundly different from present ones. Let us try to imagine it without the veil of an easy rhetoric, this isolated world that lacked running water, sanitary facilities and electricity, badly heated and with the uncertain and dangerous light from the fireplace, candles, and oil lamps. Echoing with the lowings and bleatings of livestock, the voices of men, women and children during the day, but dilating in the silence of the starry nights broken by the barking of dogs. In wintertime people gathered in the large kitchens or in the stables to keep warm: women tended to small chores, and children tried not to fall asleep in order not to miss hearing the stories, entertaining or terrifying, but all equally marvellous. Age-old therapeutic remedies, proverbs and spells were passed on. And there were songs: about love and work, nostalgia and political passion, hope and anger. This was the world that we revisit in the pages imbued with paternalistic nostalgia of *Fattoria nel Chianti* by Maria Bianca Viviani della Robbia, an aristocratic landowner; a world that in the last chapters, in the years of the late 1950s, appears already profoundly changed. The crisis of sharecropping and the politicization of the countryside, the call of the city with its factories, the abandonment of the farms, the disappearance of old customs and the megalopolitan myths of the masses had altered the fabric of peasant life, marked as it was by poverty and hard work, torn between a close attachment to traditions and the recognition of the practical utility of new techniques and new systems of land management.

The art of basketry.

Humble trades

Chianti was poor and hard-working before the advent of machinery which profoundly affected rhythms of life and working methods. Farmers knew when and how to cultivate vines, they knew the names of the various grapes and the techniques used to tend the vineyards. The "governo", entrusted to the cellarman, was often carried out under the supervision of the "capo bastone", who presided over the first pressing of the grapes, using a thick pole, and established the percentages. Even in the 1930s, with the exception of a few companies, wine paid for "sul barile", or on delivery, was transported on horse-drawn carts on which up to 800 flasks at a time were stacked – with oil and a little paper hat, a protection of straw and at times a cloth cover – in the characteristic "cesta" shaped like an upturned pyramid.

The miller, who had direct relations with the owners and large farmers, took care of the milling of grain and animal feed, and in the literary tradition was unpopular owing to the money he was accused of easily accumulating by taking advantage of the small farmer. On large estates with a good number of farms, forests, arable lands and pastures, there was often a furnace. And yet the absence of main roads and the pitiful state of local ones limited the trade in construction materials, that were above all destined for the maintenance of farm houses and agricultural buildings on the property.

However much it played an essential role in the diet of the farmer, to whom it supplied the necessary

The old cart for the transportation of wine flasks.

amount of sugars, in the Chianti of former times wine occupied a secondary position compared to cereals, which were necessary to nourish the large urban and rural population. The most advanced agricultural system was the triennial crop rotation, which ensured that the land remained fertile. From the farms, sacks of grain loaded on heavy ox-drawn carts, and large casks of wine and oil transported by mules, supplied the local markets which, for the inhabitants of the farms and villages scattered throughout the hills, were the most important events of the week. Shops were scarce and itinerant traders prospered, despite the dangers of the road: eggs, chickens, rabbits, as well as utensils and fabrics and everything that could be useful to a poor and isolated life.

Although the sharecropping contract was officially abolished in 1967, farmers had already been rejecting it for some time. When the "economic miracle" arrived in the late 1950s and early 1960s it created new opportunities for rural labourers who had no hesitation in abandoning their farm houses in search of work that was less exhausting, with more humane working hours and better pay.

The old landowners were unable to sustain the transition: farms which for centuries had been an unrenounceable patrimony of the Tuscan nobility – a life-style more than an economic investment – were taken over by a new class of entrepreneurial owners very often from other regions, who salvaged them with massive transfusions of capital, solid oenological knowledge and an impulsive desire to experiment and improve. Later the oenologists, the consultants and the winemakers arrived. But that is another story.

In the vineyard

The vineyards and vines of Chianti have by now changed their appearance: they occupy the land with different geometries, they rest on artificial supports, they exhibit new forms of clusters and leaves, new names, new colours. And yet, in this "new Tuscan Renaissance" there is still room for the old: this is evident here and there by the return to winemaking in wooden casks and the introduction of technologies which simulate grape-crushing by foot and by hand. But it is revealed above all by the reappraisal of abandoned vine plants such as Colorino, Canaiolo, Ciliegiolo and Mammolo, and the specialized revival of Sangiovese, a variety preferred for its enormous potential. As regards technical progress, however, two developments were decisive in the renewal of

A moment of the grape-harvest.

vineyards and cellars. The first, dating from the 1960s and 1970s, was flanked by a gradual yet fundamental change in oenological typology whose causes can be identified both in the diminishing of the range of low-quality products and in the necessary adaptation of the organoleptic characteristics of traditional wines to the demands of national and international markets, and also in the creation of new wines. And yet even this was still not enough. The varieties planted, in fact, included varieties of white and black grapes (especially Sangiovese, but also Canaiolo, Trebbiano, Malvasia and, in certain areas like the Pisan area, also Colorino, Mammolo and San Colombano) whose vine plants, selected with very different criteria from those of today, were often of a poor quality. The vineyards were mixed, and there was not only an excessive amount of space between rows resulting in a high unitary production that was particularly disastrous for Sangiovese, but white-grape and black-grape varieties were also aligned next to each other. Now, even in respect of the 1967 regulations concerning the numerical ratio between the vines to be planted in each vineyard, the greater productivity of Trebbiano compared to black-grape vines and especially Sangiovese, determined the presence in the grape mixture, in addition to too abundant complementary black grapes, of excessive quantities of white grapes. Such that, eluding in practice both the indications of Ricasoli and the production regulations, almost all wines, from those ready to drink to those for ageing, were made with high percentages of white grapes. What resulted was a lively though rather light wine, lacking structure and high in acidity, having a medium colour with a tendency to turn yellow, acid and tannic in the aroma, and with little body or roundness. In other words, the vines of those years produced fragrant table wines that were agreeable and easy to drink, but were not particularly highly appreciated by the wider international market: the result was that exports collapsed, the quantity of wine stocks increased enormously and prices plummeted.

A serious solution to the problem got underway around the middle of the 1980s, when changes in habits and lifestyles, new healthier diets aimed at eliminating or at least reducing daily consumptions of high-calory foods, increased economic well-being and a broader understanding of the world of wine determined the creation of a market demand that became increasingly oriented toward high-quality products. With the establishment of a new “drinking culture”, wine was no longer considered a necessary food supplement for manual workers, nor as an unrenounceable luxury for the less elevated social classes, but as a special drink to be shown off at exhibitions, to package in refined bottles, to serve in sophisticated glasses, to savour with ritual gestures, to talk about and discuss with highly specialized language, to "contemplate" in quiet and relaxing circumstances.

It was therefore the need to find new commercial outlets and to re-exploit "Chianti" with the idea of obtaining its promotion to DOCG status (1984) which induced producers to proceed with the renewal and renovation of now old-fashioned vineyards, utilizing new cultural, technical and regulation-oriented criteria that were functional to the quality of the product and were accompanied by efficient systems of commercialization. The new vineyards provided for a higher density of plantation (4000-6000 plants per hectare, while in the past they had reached 3300) with systems of rearing and pruning that were suited to them, greater attention to the tending of sloping terrains and to drainage, weaker vine stocks, the thinning out of grape clusters to prevent excessive productivity, more balanced fertilization, pest and disease control, mechanized pruning, but above all the choice of selected clones. It was, in fact, the great emphasis on the clonal selection of vines that brought about a turning-point in vine-growing in the 1990s, based on the search for ideal clones suited to that micro-environment which is Chianti, those which have the potential to characterize the vine species – at the same time guaranteeing the vigour of the plant, the type of bunch, the right balance of aromatic substances and polyphenolic complexes, the resistance to disease and the absence of virosis – and therefore the wine in terms of optimum organoleptic characteristics. Products were therefore created to be included in the DOC, DOCG and "indicazione geografica" type of wines, obtained with the use of a reconsidered Sangiovese, wines often matured in barriques and for long periods aged in the bottle.

According to the latest production regulations, Chianti Classico can be made either with 100% Sangiovese or with "recommended or authorized" black-grape vines. Thus, in addition to the traditional

The grape-harvest.
Strict quality controls are carried out in the vineyard.

Chianti vine species, more widespread use in recent years has been made of such international varieties as Cabernet Sauvignon and Merlot, explanting white-grape varieties in favour of Sangiovese or other black-grape varieties or diverting them toward other productions.

One of the results of this change, in the field of production, was the creation in 1980, by a limited number of wineries, of "Galestro", an innovation which reflected the new tastes of a certain group of consumers oriented toward light refreshing drinks to be consumed especially during the summer months. A Chianti wine even in the choice of its name, that of the grey rock that is extremely common in the area, it blended in varying proportions traditional grapes like Trebbiano, Malvasia and white Canaiolo with such noble grapes as Pinot, Chardonnay, Sauvignon, Riesling and others, harvested early, made into wine at low temperatures, and bottled

For the grape-harvest the human hand is irreplaceable.

cold to maintain its freshness and vivacity. In the same way, the new noble black-grape vines, which from 1984 could not enter into the grape mixtures of "Chianti", have allowed wineries to produce other types of wine: on the one hand light, refreshing, fruity red wines suitable for drinking young, already on the market in the spring following the harvest, and on the other hand wines of prestige obtained by mixing their grapes with those of Sangiovese, a variety often successfully vinified on its own. Let us now look at them on the vine, the four leading Chianti grapes that shine translucently, together with other "uve dei Medici", on the canvases of the Medicean painter Bartolomeo Bimbi (1648-1729), as well as the two new international black-grape vine plants allowed by the most recent regulations.

SANGIOVESE

Sangioveto, Sangiovese (or Sangiovese grosso) di Toscana, Sangiovese chiantigiano.

The Sangiovese cluster is dense and compact, conical, of medium size, often winged, and hangs from strong vine shoots that are resistant to disease. The berries are elongated, pruinous and swollen, with a dark-purplish skin, both light and substantial at the same time, the pulp not too fleshy, acidulous and pinkish. The compactness of the cluster causes rotting in particularly wet years, a not uncommon occurrence since its traditional areas are typified by frequent rains in late September and early October. From the year 2000, new vines obtained from seven approved clones (whose repetitivity in time is certified and guaranteed) have been planted by the Consorzio in the Chianti Classico area, resulting in the production of open-clustered Sangiovese grapes that are immune from the above-mentioned problem. The vine prefers dry, well-exposed clayey-siliceous-calcareous soils which are necessary to produce the sugars that soften its natural harshness. Its origins are ancient, possibly Tuscan, although on different soils it will produce different wines. Often mixed with other varieties to obtain a smoother, rounder wine, if used on its own it produces a wine of an intense ruby-red colour, tannic and full-bodied, with the fragrance of wild violets, iris and raspberry, and an intense flavour with an agreeably bitter finish that with ageing acquires nobility.

CANAIOLO

Canaiolo nero (or nero grosso), Canaiolo toscano.

The elongated, conical, short-winged, medium-sized, rather loose cluster, hanging from a sturdy peduncle, has oval-shaped, juicy grapes with a thin, dark, purply skin. Its once considerable importance has progressively waned for a number of reasons: first of all for its poor adaptability to the "piede americano" (American root stalk), widely adopted throughout Europe to protect vines from phylloxera, a ripening time that is even later than that of Sangiovese, and the low resistance of its thin skin to autumnal rains. Unblended with other grapes, it produces an elegant, fruity, less tannic wine than Sangiovese, a variety combined with it precisely to confer smoothness and agreeability.

Trebbiano

Trebbiano toscano.

Two wings protrude from this cylindrical, medium-sized, loose cluster of fairly large round grapes whose pruinous amber-yellow skin encloses a juicy sweet-acid flesh. It hangs from long, sturdy vine shoots, takes root easily and gives a high yield, especially in hilly, limestone-rocky-clayey soils. Although favouring a hot climate and dry, rich and pasty soil, it grows especially well in calcareous soil like galestro or galestrino. It combines well with any other type of grape but, when used on its own, gives a wine of a pale yellow, greenish or golden colour, with a subtle perfume of acacia, oak or strawberry tree flowers, a lively, dry consistency, pungent and harmonious, though not very characteristic. Fomerly, in Tuscany, a special white wine called "Trebbiano dolce" was made.

MALVASIA BIANCA LUNGA DEL CHIANTI
Malvasia del Chianti, Malvasia toscana.

Its name comes from the large, elongated, thick, winged pyramidal cluster, with round golden grapes having pruinous skin and juicy flesh of a medium consistency. The bunch hangs from strong shoots resistant to disease, apart from mildew, with an abundant and constant yield especially in siliceous or clayey-limestone soil that is not too humid and is well exposed to the sun. Of uncertain origin, it always seems to have been grown in Tuscany, such that many consider it to have originated here. On its own, it produces a pale yellow white wine of good body, slightly aromatic, refined, pungent, smooth, with a high alcohol content and limited acidity. With Trebbiano it makes an excellent dry white wine. From 2005 allowed only in the grapes used to make Vinsanto.

CABERNET SAUVIGNON

A highly-prized black-grape vine particularly widespread in France, in the area of Bordeaux; it reaches excellent production levels if planted in stony soils. The medium-sized clusters are few and their openness allows a degree of air circulation that defends them from the risk of rotting. The grapes themselves are smallish and juicy with a fairly thick skin and therefore very rich both in colourants and tannins. A grape which in Tuscany is harvested at the beginning of September, strictly depending on the degree of maturation, on whose agreeability the temperate climate has a positive influence. Used together with Sangiovese from the middle of the 1970s, it has been increasingly appreciated ever since.

MERLOT

A black-grape vine, also from the Bordeaux region, it can be grown in heavy, clayey soils that are hardly suited to Cabernet, from which it differs for a richer production of fruits. The clusters are smallish, as are the berries, whose compactness exposes them to the risk of rotting; a risk, however, that is reduced by its early ripening (in Tuscany it is harvested in late August, early September) which also makes it suitable for fairly cool climates. Its dark, relatively unacidic juice, rich in extracts and substance but with less aggressive tannins, makes it particularly suitable for combining with Sangiovese and Cabernet from which it removes roughness and austerity, although it is also appreciated when used on its own.

"Bacchus amat colles"

Let us now attempt to identify the production area of "Chianti Classico", established by the above-mentioned interministerial decree of July 31, 1932, for which the production of the entire communes of Castellina in Chianti, Gaiole in Chianti, Radda in Chianti, Greve in Chianti and part of the communes of Castelnuovo Berardenga, Poggibonsi, Barberino Val d'Elsa, Tavarnelle in Val di Pesa and San Casciano in Val di Pesa was authorized to use the name of "Chianti Classico", while for certain hill areas of the provinces of Siena, Florence, Arezzo, Pistoia and Pisa only the word "Chianti" was allowed.

"Chianti Classico" is produced, therefore, in the approximately 70,000 hectares distributed over the slopes of the hills covered with vineyards between Florence and Siena. An area naturally suited to the production of quality wines by virtue of its climate (continental, with moderate temperature fluctuations in the course of twenty-four hours), the accentuated altitude and the nature of the soil. And since it is, above all, the latter which influences the quality of the grapes, it is the rich presence of small stones underneath the great variety of the soils of Chianti – from the marl of the area of San Casciano to the calcareous-clayey soil of Greve, to the sandstone of the mountains, to the alberese of the mid south, to the tufa of Castelnuovo Berardenga – which enables the production of a vast range of wines of varying bouquet, body, alcohol content, although all of them limpid, a fine lively ruby-red, turning to garnet with ageing, with a winey odour perfumed with violets and a pronounced delicacy in the ageing phase, harmonious, dry, pungent and slightly tannic taste, which becomes velvety smooth in the course of time. The operations of vinification, conservation, bottling and refining in the bottle and ageing must be carried out within the production area; while the making available for consumption is allowed exclusively in glass containers appropriate for a prized wine and, should it be bottled in flasks, only in new traditional Tuscan ones. In both cases, with the exception of containers with a capacity of less than 0.25 litres, the use of a cork stopper is strictly prescribed. The elegance of "Chianti Classico" goes perfectly well with the traditional Florentine beefsteak, and with cheeses, while the full-bodiedness of the "Riserva" demands a fine roast lamb, stewed rabbit or mature cheeses... and can make it an excellent wine "for contemplation".

In the wine cellar

The geological origin of the land, the climate, the exposure, and the selection of the vine plants are not enough to make a great wine. The hand of man is indispensable: humble, skilled hands, which even after the advent of machinery tend to the pruning, to the tying of the vine shoots and to the gathering of the bunches of grapes; the expert hands of technicians that work the clonic selection of the various vines to produce high quality, that control the ripening of the grapes for a better sugar content, the right acidity and the appropriate colour and aroma. And they experiment with new methods of fermentation and drawing off of the wine.

The advent of new vineyard owners in Chianti brought a dramatic situation to light. Not only were the vineyards badly cultivated and the wine badly produced, but a generation of non-existent investments left a legacy of old and dilapidated equip-

Hopper.

ment: plaster ruined by mildew, encrusted barrels (which at their best acted as inert containers, but which invariably transferred their bitterness to the wine), badly lined and cracked fermentation casks and, almost everywhere, colonies of bacteria nourished by dreadful hygiene.

Particularly hard to die was the conviction that old casks were vital in improving the quality of the wine and it was necessary to go through the not very happy experience of the scraping of their staves which involved removing from their inner surface almost a centimetre of wood until finding the layer not yet "exhausted" by wine before the use of new and smaller oak casks was accepted (from 1500-2000 litres, up to a maximum of 4000-5000), to which would subsequently be added the small 225-litre barriques. At the other extreme, of course, was the fact that, attacked by the new wood, wines poor in extractive substances and lacking in aroma lost their organoleptic characteristics.

Completely different also the criteria with which new cellars were built. The introduction, in partial substitution of cement vats, of metal casks initially with a fairly small diameter and therefore usually coming in fairly tall shapes, initially in enamelled iron and later in stainless steel (at times even in fibre-glass) which, besides not giving off substances that were unpleasant or even harmful to the wine, to one's health or to the palate, were practically indestructable and permitted the fermentation temperature to be regulated, determined in fact changes even in the realm of architecture. Thus began the work of improving, replacing, modifying, creating more appropriate environments and introducing machinery more suited to correct wine-making that were abreast of the times, like pressers and stem-separating machines which were more in keeping with the new concept of soft and delicate pressing; more advanced techniques were adopted to get the most out of the skins (prized wines must, in fact, macerate for longer in contact with them) and to proceed with an extractive operation of the skins – where the true quality of the wine resides – which favoured the release of the coloured substances, the aroma and the taste, avoiding the formation of dregs resulting from their disintegration; selected yeasts were used (which are found naturally in the skins, but which can also be added in the cellar) which could regulate the alcoholic fermentation, aimed at transforming the sugars present in the must into alcohol and carbon dioxide, taking care that this happened at the right temperatures; by means of bacterial cultures there followed malolactic fermentation which, by transforming malic acid into the gentler and more delicate lactic acid, reduced the overall level of acidity, preventing the production of astringent and sour sensations on the palate, and better developed the organoleptic characteristics of the various wines.

Lastly, the system of ageing was changed by adopting the evolution in wood and the refinement in glass. At one time, in fact, it was firmly believed that this should happen in contact with air, that is, before the wine passed into the containers or the vats. And the wines of former times, more tannic, oxidized without an excessive loss of flavour, taking on a beautiful brick-orange hue. Today, instead, wine is aged protected from contact with the air, in hermetically sealed bottles or barrels to safeguard not

Wine left to age in barriques.

only the flavour and aroma, but also the colour. And that is not all: if maturation in wood stabilizes the structure of the wine and smooths out roughness and harshness through a slow and controlled process of gasey exchanges, ageing in bottles also favours the formation of the bouquet, a delicate blend of aromas that are labile and sensitive to oxygen. The most robust wines should stay longer in the casks, but only the richest of them can tolerate the enveloping contact of the barrique. During ageing in wood, which chronologically comes after malolactic fermentation, it is necessary to pour off the wine at regular intervals to free it of sediments and prevent the formation of unpleasant odours.

The ideal cellar today has large well-exposed rooms (north-facing those for ageing in casks and bottling), at least partially underground, with the right amount of natural light, efficient air circulation and a

A pleasant area of the wine-cellar for "meditation".

constant temperature, walls and floors resistant to seepage and strong enough to be able to support the weight of casks, vats and tanks, as well as all the equipment and machinery. At times it is necessary to install ventilation systems, and screens at the windows to prevent insects and rodents from entering, to rapidly eliminate the residue of the must, the liquid and solid dregs, the mildew and all the substances that could contaminate either the rooms or the wine. Above all, water should be available for the hygiene of the workers and for washing, and drains for waste disposal.

An ideal domestic wine cellar also needs thick walls, a healthy permeable floor, no lights, no noise, good circulation, at least 80% humidity and a constant temperature of between 10° and 15°. With the bottles on shelves possibly made of wood so as not to transfer to the bottles the vibrations of road traffic, far from the walls to favour the circulation of air, as also from sources of heat and from smells that the

wine might absorb, in a horizontal position to permit the dampened cork to adhere better to the glass with the aim of preventing oxidations that are violent and disagreeable to the palate, and the highest places reserved for red wines which – since warm air tends to rise – need higher temperatures than whites or rosés.
Today even the "strapeso" flask of Laborel, which up until the 1950s was one of the most well-known receptacles in the world given that it formed part of

the baggage of Italian emigrants, is becoming rare. Picturesque, it is true, and of ancient tradition too since we can identify two of them tied to the wrists of the maidservant proudly striding in with a tray of fruit on her head, painted by Ghirlandaio (1449-1494) in the church of Santa Maria Novella in Florence. And yet, in the long run, it was frowned upon due to the uneconomical space it occupied in the wine cellar and was unpopular because it contributed to the spread of a rustic, tav-

The horizontal position of the bottle prevents the premature drying of the cork stopper.

erny image for a wine that was getting ready to move up with those of a higher quality. The bottle, therefore, is the most appropriate environment for storing wine after the long labours connected with its transformation from grape juice to enological product, enabling it to carry out slowly and with all due tranquillity the final physical and chemical changes. There are bottles of various capacity and various forms; but Chianti Classico requires the "bordolese" made of dark glass, given that light and ultraviolet rays interfere negatively on the ageing of the product.

Today there are also various types of stopper, each of which has its own particular virtue in watching over the correct rest of the wine; however, for a wine destined for ageing cork stoppers are indispensable, elegant and unquestionably good-looking. And precious too, when you consider the long process of drying, boiling and rest in fresh air necessary before being able to cut them into smooth flexible little cylinders. Completely disappeared, instead, in favour of thin aluminium covers, the heavy caps of lead alloy, pleasantly malleable, but responsible for contaminating the wine with substances extremely harmful to human health.

On the table

It may perhaps be superfluous to mention, but the label is today more than ever before the passport of the wine, imposed by Italian law which makes compulsory the indication of the category to which it belongs (for example whether it is sparkling or not, if a table wine, with a geographical indication, and/or with an indication of the vine, DOC, DOCG), its alcohol content, the country it comes from, the name of the bottler, and the capacity of the bottle. The year and the production area are obligatory only for DOC and DOCG wines, and the containers of the latter should have a capacity not exceeding 5 litres and bear a sign released on the basis of approval by the Chamber of Commerce which, on every single batch of wine, carries out a chemical analysis in respect of the parameters provided for by the regulations and an organoleptic assessment, in other words, a tasting. Only after this approval, in fact, the wine finally becomes "Chianti Classico" and can be bottled. With the notice that to "Chianti Classico" only the specification "Riserva" is allowed. In this case the emblem of the Gallo Nero placed on the neck of the bottle, instead of the red border typical of young production, will have the characteristic golden border. Nonetheless, to be absolutely sure of what you are about to drink, the only way is to see it, smell it, but above all taste it.

Opening a bottle of wine is an art that requires some care in order to avoid breaking the cork, an accident that is all the more likely if the cork has remained in contact with the wine for some years. For this purpose one can rely on an unimaginable array of special corkscrews (recommended are those with a single levering arm which, being smaller and therefore easier to handle, require the use of a single hand while the other hand holds the bottle), grippers, methods that always enable the expert to succeed. More elaborate, on the other hand, is decanting into an appropriate carafe, called a decanter, generally considered to be indispensable for all aged red wines; and yet this is true only for mature wines still in the fullness of their strength, ones which run no risk of oxidizing rapidly. Often it is not enough to leave a bottle for a few days in an upright position to get the sediment to sink to the bottom. After having brought the bottle to room temperature, the protective cap is cut just below the ring of glass surrounding the neck, the upper part is removed and the cork and rim of the neck are cleaned to remove any mould or dirt that may have

Tasting wine in the glass allows one to fully appreciate the bouquet of Chianti Classico.

formed. Then, without agitating the bottle, the cork is removed without piercing it entirely so as to avoid cork fragments falling into the wine, the rim of the neck is cleaned of any cork dust and the cork itself is checked by smelling it and observing it carefully to get a first impression of the wine's state of conservation. Then the wine is gently poured into a carafe, this too at room temperature, watching through the glass the approach of the sediment toward the neck of the bottle. The slow contact with air produces a light oxygenation, favouring the development of the enclosed aromas of the old wine which will also become smoother to the taste. At this point, the wine close to senescence should be consumed immediately so as not to risk acescence and the flattening of the perfumes.

Fundamental for a correct tasting of "Chianti Classico" is a good glass, completely transparent with a fairly broad round base, with a long slender stem to hold between the index finger and the thumb (perhaps also the middle finger) to prevent possible odours present on the hand from mixing with that of the wine and the bowl of a shape that recalls a tulip (narrow at the base, wider in the middle, and narrowing slightly at the rim) to allow the perfumes to be released into the air before being channelled towards the nose. Filled to about a third full, it should then be swirled in the glass to allow the wine to best express its aromas.

Even at the table the glass used for an important "Classico", aged for a few years, should be filled no more than two-thirds full and must be of generous proportions, although the diameter of the glass decreases progressively as one passes to structured Chiantis and those of a certain maturity, to young elegant wines, and finally to young wines of a medium structure, or light ones having little tannin, of which instead they should emphasize the aroma and the qualities of fruitiness and freshness. Glasses should be washed with warm water and very little soap, dried immediately, and stored standing up. They should be rewashed if they have been standing too long in a cabinet (glasses easily absorb the odour of furniture) and can even be flavoured with a drop of the wine that is to be served in them.

Before actually introducing the wine into the mouth, the tasting is carried out with the eyes and the nose. First of all we should observe the clearness of the wine, and to do this correctly, we must raise the glass to the level of the eyes and then lower it over a white surface, tilting it with the base facing towards us so as to observe it against the light. Then we should examine its liveliness, intensity and colour. Even the alcohol content can be "seen" by simply rotating the glass and observing the small "tears" that form along its edges as the liquid settles again. The number of these tears and the speed with which they descend depend on the evaporation and therefore on the alcohol content of the wine.

The aromas of a wine can also be recognized by

twirling the glass and inhaling for a couple of seconds (no more, for the alcohol can inhibit the olfactory mucous); and yet, since they are volatile substances, it is inevitable that some of them will be perceived at the beginning, whereas others will be perceived only when the glass is still.

The more intense, penetrating and composite the perfumes are, the higher the quality of the wine.

Finally we can take into the mouth a small quantity of liquid,

The warm colours of the living-room in a Chianti house.

which the expert wine-taster will channel along the edges of the tongue to the back of the mouth and then return to the tip of the tongue, washing over the central part and then pressing the tongue against the palate to "break" the wine and so liberate other substances. But of course anyone can enjoy a good glass of Chianti Classico by simply swirling it around in the mouth before swallowing it: lively and rounded, harmonious and dry, pungent and slightly tannic when young, smooth and velvety at the end of a correct period of ageing, when it will give off a perfume of wild fruits and spices.

Rows of vines with olive trees.

Mal di Chianti

The enemies of the vine advance in hosts, favoured by temperature and humidity and forming among themselves inconceivable alliances. In the first row marches phylloxera and other animal parasites – moths, mites, masticating and sucking cicadas, tiny spiders, acid rot – followed by legions of bacteria and viruses which, if not actually killing the plant within a few seasons, force their destruction to prevent contagion. In the rearguard instead is the infestatious flora, both annual and perennial: rye-grass, dogwood, cankerwort, bindweed, wild mint, horsetail, artemisia, and others still. But the most substantial part of this army comprises the cryptogamic diseases: peronospora, or downy mildew (*Plasmopara viticola*), oidium, or powdery mildew (*Uncinula necator*), botrytis (*Botrytis cinerea*), and a host of secondary infections supported by fungal agents such as excoriosis and black measles.

They are called the "years of peronospora" in the phytopathological chronicles, the years of violent and relentless destruction by this fungus that works away at the vegetation of the vine and is

capable of extensive damage in climatic conditions favorable to its development. It was first seen in 1878 when, introduced to Europe from North America, it unleashed virulent attacks in numerous Italian regions, including Tuscany. After penetrating the tissue, the infection appears on the leaves as characteristic "oil stains" and then as a whitish mildew. Soon the infected area becomes yellow, the leaves wither and fall, and the bunches of grapes are irreparably damaged. Defense against it was first identified as a preventive treatment with a mixture of copper sulphate and lime (the "Bordeaux mixture"); at the end of the 1940s this was substituted by organic antimildew products and in 1980 by the first endotherapic antimildew fungicide.

Another scourge, oidium or "white mildew", which also spread to Europe by infected vines imported from America (1845), is instead responsible for two types of damage: one direct, consisting of the falling of the flowers and newly-formed grape-berries and the splitting of these during growth so that their normal development is prevented; and an indirect one whereby, like the grape-berry moths, it promotes the devastating action of "gray mildew". Oidium is a fungus that thrives at temperatures between 25° and 28°, while its diffusion is hindered by continual rains and high atmospheric humidity, and it detests sulphur-based treatments with which it has been combated effectively since the signs of its first appearance in Europe.

On the contrary, botrytis or "gray mildew" became increasingly harmful from the 1960s due to the increase in intensive techniques applied to cultivation and to the partial abandonment of copper salts due to the development of antimildew defenses. It develops in the spring, in suitable conditions of temperature but in particular of atmospheric humidity, although the devastation becomes apparent at harvest time, when rains are more frequent and the grape-berries, at an advanced stage of maturation, are more vulnerable.

Hail, hoarfrost and freezing weather, especially when out of season, complete the picture of natural calamities that have always endangered the plants, the grapes, the very essence of this corner of the world that is called Chianti.

Chianti Classico

DOCG Decree 05/08/1996 - G.U. 18/09/1996.
Replacing D.P.R. of 02/07/1984.

Production area:
the same established by Interministerial Decree 31/07/1932, confirmed by D.P.R. 12/07/1963, 09/08/1967 and 02/07/1984. The area – extending for roughly 70,000 hectares over hilly terrain with a maximum altitude of 700 m asl, with arenaceous, marny-calcareous, argillaceous, sandy and stoney substrata – is situated between the two provinces of Florence and Siena, including in their entirety the communes of Castellina in Chianti, Radda in Chianti, Gaiole in Chianti, Greve in Chianti; part of the communes of San Casciano in Val di Pesa, Barberino Val d'Elsa, Tavarnelle Val di Pesa, Castelnuovo Berardenga; a small part of the commune of Poggibonsi.

Note: in the vinification are permitted only local practices allowed by the laws in force, including the traditional enological practice of "governo all'uso toscano", which consists of a slow refermentation of the just drawn-off wine with slightly dried grapes.

Denomination	Other types	Yield in quintals per hectare	Ageing in months
Chianti Classico	–	75 (grape yield in wine 70%)	from October 1 of the year followi the grape harves
Chianti Classico	Riserva	75 (grape yield in wine 70%)	at least 24 mont from January 1 af the grape harve (of which at least the bottle)

Vines: Sangiovese 80-100%; complementary black-grape vines, recommended or authorized in the production areas, up to a maximum of 20%; Trebbiano toscano and Malvasia bianca, either singly or together, up to 6% (though only up to the harvest of 2005 inclusive).

Production limits: in favourable years it cannot exceed 20% of the production allowed, under penalty of declassification. However, in exceptional years this limit can be lowered with the issuing of a regional decree.

Grape yield in wine: the surplus between 70% and 75% has no right to be a DOC wine; beyond this percentage limit all production is down-graded to table wine.

Production controls: both in the vineyard and in the cellar before and during the harvest.

Vinification, bottling, conservation and ageing: all to be carried out within the production area. DOCG wine can be made available for consumption only in containers with a capacity of less than 5 l and must be sealed with a State countermark that is proof of the controls that have been effected.

Eligibility to DOCG Chianti Classico status: every batch of wine must come from vineyards registered at the Albo and must fulfil the requirements of a rigorous chemical and organoleptic analysis.

Organoleptic characteristics: clear, lively, ruby-red colour tending to garnet with ageing; vinous perfume with a scent of wild violets and with a pronounced finesse in the ageing phase; harmonious, dry, sapid and slightly tannic in flavour, with time turning to a velvety smoothness.
The "governo" confers vivacity and roundness.

lcohol content	Minimum total acidity	Minimum dry extract
12%	4.5 grams per litre	23 grams per litre
12,5%	4.5 grams per litre	23 grams per litre

GALLO NERO STANDARD

Year	Quality	Average alcohol	Total acidity	Colour intensity	Dry extract
1991	***	12,60	–	▲	▲
good body and colour, suitable for medium ageing					
1992	**	12,40	–/▼	–	–
little colour, less structure than usual, pleasant flavour					
1993	****	12,70	–	▲	–
intense colour, excellent perfume, for medium to long ageing					
1994	***	12,80	–/▼	▲	–
good colour, ample perfume, smooth, harmonious flavour, for normal ageing					
1995	*****	13	–/▲	▲	▲
very intense colour, excellent perfume, sapid, for long ageing					
1996	****	12,72	–	–	–/▲
good body and colour, sapid, excellent perfume, harmonious flavour, for medium to long ageing					
1997	*****	13,24	–/▲	–	▲
full-bodied and with good colour, sapid, perfumed, particularly suitable for long ageing					
1998	****	12,90	–	▲	–/▲
good body and colour, sapid, fine perfume, harmonious flavour, suitable for medium ageing					
1999	*****	13,10	–	–/▲	▲
full-bodied, with good colour, robust, sapid, suitable for long ageing					
2000	****	12,80	–	–/▲	–/▲
intense flavour, perfumed, for medium to long ageing					
2001	**	13,17	–/▼	–	▲
good body and colour, harmonious flavour, for medium ageing					
2002	**	12,62	▲	–/▲	–
medium body and colour, agreeable flavour, for short ageing					

LEGENDA

** good
*** very good
**** excellent
***** exceptional

Total acidity
▼ low, less than 5.50 g/l in tartaric acid
– medium, between 5.50 and 6.50 g/l in tartaric acid
▲ high, more than 6.50 g/l in tartaric acid

Colour intensity
▼ low, less than 3.50 g/l expressed in Sudraud index
– medium, between 3.50 and 5,50 expressed in Sudraud index
▲ high, more than 5.50 g/l expressed in Sudraud index

Dry extract
▼ low, less than 24.50 g/l
– medium, between 24.50 and 26.00 g/l
▲ high, more than 26.00 g/l

Glossary

Acidity
A fundamental quality in a wine. If acidity is lacking, the wine will be characterless; if in excess, it will be sharp on the palate and nose (see freshness).

Affinamento
The maturing and ageing process used with the aim of giving a wine balanced organoleptic qualities.

Ampelography
The science that studies vines and different varieties of grape.

Aroma
The smell of young wines that have not developed the complexity of the bouquet.

Asciutto
Dry, sober, straightforward wine with even character.

Astringent
Wine that leaves the palate feeling dry and rough, usually caused by excessive acidity and a high tannin content.

Austere
Wine with a high alcohol content and a good amount of tannin, qualities which promise the further acquisition of agreeability and expressiveness.

Balanced
Wine in which extract, tannins, acidity, effervescence, alcohol and smoothness coexist in the right and harmonious proportions.

Barriques
Small casks of an elongated form, originally from Bordeaux, once used both for the ageing and transportation of wine. Widespread in Italy especially over the last fifty years, they have often replaced larger traditional casks. Even today containers of the same shape, though having a greater capacity (225 l) than the traditional ones, are incorrectly called barriques.

Body
The general gustatory sensations of a wine in terms of robustness, richness and concentration.

Bouquet
The aromas and perfumes of a wine, to which ageing has conferred depth and complexity.

Cask
Wooden container used for ageing wine, once having a capacity varying between 10 and 100 hectolitres, today generally between 45 and 50.

Cappello
The layer of skins, pips and stems that forms in the upper part of the vat, pushed to the surface by carbon dioxide released by the fermentation of sugars.

Chewy
Wine of a rather dense consistency, rich in glycerin, although generally well-balanced.

Clarification
Operation preliminary to bottling, used to eliminate any material suspended in the wine and confer clearness and brilliance.

Clone
Group of organisms coming from a single vine variety by means of various types of asexual reproduction. Clonal selection allows identifying the qualitatively best vines in order to reproduce them in the nursery.

Complexity
The overall aromatic and gustatory characteristics of a wine, usually accentuated and enriched with ageing in the bottle.

Concentrated
Wine of considerable body and extract resulting from an excellent maturation and a correct fermentation of the grapes.

Delicate
Applies to wines that are light, young and fresh.

Development
Capacity of a wine to express different, complex and well-balanced aspects of its character.

Diraspatura
Operation preliminary to pressing consisting of separating the grape berries from their stems.

Disciplinare di produzione
The code of regulations, set out in a specific decree, regulating the production of a DOC wine as regards name, vine type, grape yield per hectare, capacity of containers, labelling, etc.

DOC
Denominazione di origine controllata (Denomination of controlled origin).

DOCG
Denominazione di origine controllata e garantita (Denomination of controlled and guaranteed origin).

Elegant
Wine of great class, with elevated qualities, merits and characteristics not easily found in other wines.

Finish
Flavour impression left in the mouth after swallowing.

Herbaceous
An olfactory and gustatory sensation of cut grass which, if of moderate proportions, broadens the aromatic spectrum of a wine.

Extract
The entire range of colouring substances, tannins, mineral salts, stable acids, albuminoids, glycerin and pectin, whose richness defines a wine of quality.

Dregs
Deposit or sediment that collects on the bottom of the cask during the ageing of a wine, contributing to conferring body and fullness.

Fermentation
Process of transformation worked by yeasts present in the sugars contained in the grape, which transform them into alcohol and carbon dioxide.

Fermentation vat
Large open container, usually conical in shape, used for the fermentation of the must. At one time made of wood, they have gradually been substituted by stainless steel tanks.

Follatura
An operation consisting of pressing down the pomace suspended in the fermentation vat. Formerly carried out with poles, today it is usually done by the pistons the vats are equipped with.

Fragrant
Wine with an agreeable smell of fruits and herbs.

Fresh
Characteristic of young wines with the right balance of acidity and fruitiness.

Fruity
Wine in which the smell of grapes is dominant. Quality wines are fruity when young, assuming greater complexity once aged.

Glycerin
Or glycerol. Present in great quantity in important wines, it is produced during fermentation, giving roundness to the wine.

Harmonious
Wine in which the taste components are perfectly balanced.

IGT
Indicazione geografica tipica.

Lively
Quality wine, agreeable to the palate and of constant acidity.

Maceration
Process immediately after fermentation, in which the liquid part is kept in contact with the cake of skins, pips and stems, etc.

Noble
Vineyard, vine or wine with well-defined characteristics superior to the norm.

Oxidation
Phenomenon present in wines that have reached the final stage of their development, though also when they have been left for too long in contact with the air in an open bottle or closed by a cork that fails to seal efficiently. However, it can

also be caused by incorrect vinification: the colour becomes burnished, the perfumes fade and the taste is flat and cloying.

PERSISTENCE
The continuation of sensorial stimuli perceived after swallowing, whose duration is an indication of the quality of the wine.

PRESSING
Process of forcing the juice out of grape berries by splitting their skins and squeezing out the juice, today done with rollers instead of with the feet.

PRILLARE
The swirling of wine in the bowl of the wine-glass.

PERFUMED
Describes a young wine, generally elegant though not too full-bodied, whose fragrances derive from the type of vine or from the cask in which it ferments.

RACKING
Separation of the wine from the deposit that forms on the bottom of the cask or vat, usually carried out by means of a pump.

RICH
Quality deriving from a good presence of extract, concentration and alcohol content.

ROBUST
Well-structured wine, rich in alcohol, full in taste.

ROUND
Wine with good body, smooth tannins and balanced acidity.

SMOOTH
Wine with low acidity, good body and roundness, not aggressive and with smooth tannins.

STRUCTURED
Wine rich in extract, with good concentration, perceptible tannins and balanced acidity.

TABLE WINE
It occupies the lowest level in the hierarchy of Italian wines. If at one time it often included innovative wines of a reasonable quality, lacking denomination of origin status (DOC and DOCG), after the entry of IGT wines they are generally limited to the most current productions.

TANNIC
Wine with a strong presence of tannins which produce a pronounced sensation of astringency, agreeable when in balance with other components, but unpleasant when in excess.

TANNINS
The chemical substances present in skins, pips and stems which are extracted during fermentation and which contribute to the wine's longevity. In the right quantity they confer body and structure to the wine,

although when excessive they produce an impression of roughness, harshness and astringency.

VELVETY
Wine with smooth structure and round taste.

VIGOROUS
Wine with a high alcohol content and considerable character.

VINOUS
Wine with a good alcohol content, balanced even when young.

VITIGNO
Cultivated variety of vine.

YIELD PER HECTARE
The total quantity of grapes harvested in every hectare of vineyard, stipulated by the production code in the denominations of origin to guarantee a high quality of the final product. In the production regulations of "Chianti Classico", however, reference is also rightly made to the average yield of grapes per plant, which can be no higher than 3 kilos.

Recipes

N.B. The suggested quantities in these recipes are intended for 6 people, unless otherwise indicated.
For best results the use of local products is recommended: Dop Chianti Classico olive oil, Vinsanto DOC Chianti Classico, vinegar, meat, hams, salami and lard from the Siena region.

Ciccioli chiantigiani (Chianti pork scraps)

Ingredients: *fresh pork lard, extra virgin olive oil, salt.*

Cut the lard first into slices and then into pieces; brown the pieces a few at a time in a skillet with very little oil, removing them when they become golden brown. Press them well to drain off the fat and oil; the latter should be returned to the skillet to continue frying. Salt the ciccioli and eat them hot; or place them in a glass jar, cover with salt and close tightly. They can be used either with stewed meats or to make bread and tasty "schiacciate". Accompany with a rustic, robust Chianti Classico.

Salsicce chiantigiane (Chianti sausages)

Ingredients for 15 sausages: *600 g of lean pork meat, 400 g of fatty pork meat, 1 pork casing, 4 garlic cloves, 1 teaspoon of fennel seeds or others of choice (optional), 2 pinches of fresh ground pepper, 2 level tablespoons of salt.*

Finely mince the pork meat, add to it the crushed garlic, salt, pepper and spices and mix thoroughly. Put through the meat mincer again. Wash the casing, tie one end with a string and with the aid of a funnel fill it with the mixture, pressing firmly to make it compact. Tie it at intervals with string to form small sausages 7-9 cm long. Eat the sausages fresh on country bread accompanied by a good Chianti Classico, or hang them in a dry, well-ventilated place to be eaten later.

Crostini al Vinsanto (Toasted bread slices with Vinsanto)

Ingredients: *500 g of bird giblets (thrush or woodcock), 12 slices of toasted bread, 1/2 glass of Vinsanto, 1 tablespoon of capers, 1 small onion, 1 glass of broth, juice of 1 lemon, 1 bouillon cube, a pinch of grated nutmeg, 25 g of butter, 1 teaspoon of olive oil, salt, pepper.*

Clean the giblets, wash them and in a blender combine them with the capers. Sauté the thinly sliced onion in butter and oil, add the bouillon cube and the giblets and cook. When they are done, add the lemon juice, the Vinsanto and the nutmeg, correct the seasoning and mix until the mixture is creamy. Dip the bread slices rapidly into the lukewarm broth, spread the giblet mixture on them and serve.

Collo ripieno (Stuffed neck of chicken)

Ingredients for 4 people: *1 chicken neck, 2 chicken livers, 2 eggs, the "mollica" (soft part) of a bread roll, a handful of grated Parmigiano, 1 tablespoon of chopped parsley and garlic, 1 pinch of nutmeg, 1 carrot, 1 celery stalk, 1 onion, milk, salt, pepper.*

Singe, debone and clean the neck; stuff it with a mixture prepared with the minced livers, eggs, Parmigiano, the "mollica" of bread soaked in milk and squeezed, the herbs and the salt. Sew the openings closed and boil with the carrot, celery and onion, preferably in beef broth.

Ginestrata (Cinnamon broth)

Ingredients: *1/2 l of lean chicken broth, 4 fresh eggs, 1/2 glass of Vinsanto, 1 pinch of ground cinnamon, 1 pinch of grated nutmeg, 1 knob of butter (optional), 1 tablespoon of sugar (optional).*

In a bowl beat the egg yolks with the Vinsanto; add the cold broth and the cinnamon; mix, strain and heat in a saucepan. Cook, adding the butter until the mixture is slightly thickened, sprinkle with nutmeg (and sugar) and serve with a young Chianti Classico.

Risotto al Chianti (Chianti risotto)

Ingredients: *400 g of rice, 4 sausages, 1 glass of light Chianti Classico with good acidity, 2 cups of broth, 4 onions, 4 garlic cloves, grated sharp pecorino cheese, 3 tablespoons of extra virgin olive oil, salt, crushed pepper.*

Cut the onion into thin slices and brown it in the oil together with the garlic. Add the crumbled sausages, brown, add the rice, mixing well. Sprinkle with the wine and cook until it evaporates, then add the hot broth. When done, adjust the salt, add the pepper, sprinkle abundantly with the pecorino and serve with a full-bodied Chianti Classico.

Stracotto al Chianti (Chianti-style stewed beef)

Ingredients: *1200 g of stewing beef, 1 l of full-bodied Chianti Classico with good acidity, 2 zucchine, 2 carrots, 2 onions, 2 celery stalks, 1.5 l of broth, 3 tablespoons of oil, salt, 30 g of butter, 1.5 tablespoons of black peppercorns, 3 cloves.*

The day before: tie the meat with string, place it in an earthenware casserole with the oil and butter and brown it over a high flame. When the meat has browned all over add the vegetables, wine, spices and salt and bring to the boil. Cover with a lid, turn the heat right down and simmer for 6 hours, turning the meat over about once every hour. Remove from the heat and let stand overnight.

The next day; return the meat to the flame after removing the fat in the pan, add the broth and cook over a low flame until the liquid is reduced to 1 cup. Untie the meat and place it on a warm serving dish.

Strain the pan juice, pour it over the meat and serve. Accompany with a Chianti Classico Riserva.

Galletto ruspante (Farmyard chicken)

Ingredients for 4 people: *1 young farmyard chicken, 2 glasses of light Chianti Classico, 1 cup of broth, 2 teaspoons of tomato paste, 1 handful of flour, 1 handful of dry olives, 30 fresh black grapes (Sangiovese or Canaiolo), 1 sprig of rosemary, extra virgin olive oil, salt, pepper.*

Clean and singe the chicken, cut into pieces, dust with flour and brown in an earthenware pan with oil, salt, pepper and rosemary. When half done, cover with the wine and cook until it evaporates. Then add half of the broth, the tomato paste, the olives and the grapes, and cook for about 15 minutes adding the broth. Arrange the meat on a serving dish, thicken the sauce, pour it over the meat and serve with a good aged Chianti Classico.

Coniglio con olive nere chiantigiane (Rabbit with black olives)

Ingredients for 4 people: *1 young rabbit, 200 g black olives, 6 slices of toasted country bread, 1 glass of Trebbiano, 1 cup of broth, 1 onion, 1 garlic clove, 1 carrot, 1 celery stalk, vinegar, 1/2 glass of oil, salt, pepper.*

Remove and discard the viscera, wash well in water and vinegar, dry and cut into pieces. In a terracotta pan lightly brown in the oil the chopped onion and garlic, adding the carrot cut into rounds, the julienned celery and the rabbit. Add salt, pepper and cook until lightly brown. Sprinkle with wine, add the olives and cook, adding the broth a little at a time until done. Garnish with bread and serve.

Note: By doubling the sauce, you have a great sauce for fresh tagliatelle boiled in salted hot water.

Bistecchine al finocchio selvatico (Pork steaks with wild fennel seeds)

Ingredients: *6 pork steaks, 1 glass of at least a two year-old Chianti Classico, 100 g of "rigatino" (or bacon), 600 g of ripe tomatoes, 200 g of green olives, 1 onion, a handful of wild fennel seeds, 2 tablespoons of extra virgin olive oil, salt, pepper.*

Cut the onion into thin slices and fry in the oil until soft. Add and brown the chopped rigatino. Add the steaks, brown on both sides, salt, pepper and sprinkle with wine. Add the tomatoes in pieces, the olives and the fennel seeds. Cook over a low flame until the sauce thickens.

Salsa al Dragoncello (Tarragon sauce)

Ingredients: *1 handful of Siena tarragon leaves, 1 handful of basil, 2 garlic cloves, the "mollica" of one roll, Chianti vinegar, extra virgin olive oil, salt, pepper.*

Finely chop the herbs and garlic, adding the vinegar-soaked and wrung-out "mollica", a little salt and plenty of pepper. Add the oil gradually until an even, creamy mixture is formed. Store and serve with boiled meats and a good young Chianti.

Schiacciata con l'uva (Flat bread with grapes)

Ingredients: *500 g of flour, 150 g of sugar, 20 g of brewer's yeast, 800 g of black grapes, 1 handful of chopped walnuts, 1 sprig of rosemary, 6 tablespoons of extra virgin olive oil, salt.*

Make a well of the flour mixed with the sugar on the pastry board. Add the yeast that has been dissolved in lukewarm water, half of the grapes, 3 tablespoons of the oil, the chopped nuts, and a pinch of salt. Mix until a smooth ball is formed, cover and let rise for about 3 hours in a warm place away from air currents. Knead the dough again, then spread it in an oiled rectangular pan, decorate it with the remaining grapes, sprinkle with sugar and rosemary and bake in a 180° oven for 30 minutes or until done. Serve with a good young Chianti Classico.

Dolce al giaggiolo (Iris cream)

Ingredients: *200 g of ladyfingers, 3 eggs, 150 g of sugar, 2 tablespoons of flour, 1/2 l of milk, 3 tablespoons of cooking alcohol, 1 tablespoon of iris essence.*

Beat the eggs and add the sugar, flour and milk; cook in a double saucepan until the mixture becomes creamy with no lumps. Add the essence of iris to the cooking alcohol and dip the ladyfingers in the mixture. Cover the bottom of a soup tureen with half of the ladyfingers, pour the cream mixture over them and cover the cream with the remainder of the ladyfingers. Keep in a cool place until ready to serve with Vinsanto.

Pan co' Santi

Ingredients: *500 g of flour, 25 g of brewer's yeast, 100 g of walnut pieces, 100 g of sugar, 50 g of raisins, the grated rind of 1 lemon, 1 teaspoon of lard, extra virgin olive oil, 1 pinch of pepper, salt.*

Dissolve the yeast in lukewarm water and mix it with the flour and salt until a homogeneous smooth ball is formed. Cover and let rise in a warm place away from air currents. In the meantime, soak the raisins in lukewarm water and rapidly sauté the walnut pieces in the lard. When the dough has risen add the nuts, the squeezed raisins, sugar, the fresh ground pepper and lemon rind and knead until the dough is elastic. With oil-coated hands, form a small round loaf and let rise again for about 3 hours. Heat the oven to 180° and bake the bread for about 45 minutes. It will stay fresh for several days and can be eaten accompanied by new wine.

Cantucci del Chianti (Chianti dry biscuits)

Ingredients: *300 g + 3 tablespoons of flour, 200 g of sugar, 3 eggs, 50 g of toasted and chopped almonds, 50 g of toasted and chopped hazelnuts, 40 g of pine nuts, 15 g of brewer's yeast, a pinch of vanillin powder, 1 tablespoon of butter, a pinch of salt.*

Dissolve the yeast in a little lukewarm water and mix in all the ingredients. Knead and let the dough rest in a covered bowl for about 2 hours in a warm place away from air currents. Knead the dough again, and form rolls of about 4 cm in diameter. Press it down slightly and bake on a greased and floured baking sheet in a 180° oven for 30 minutes. Remove and let cool, then cut into 1 cm thick slices. Sprinkle with the sugar and return to a 160° oven for 15 minutes to toast. Serve with Vinsanto.

Bibliography

Various Authors, *Cultura contadina in Toscana*, 2 vols, Firenze 1989;

Various Authors, *L'arte e il vino in terra di Toscana*, Firenze 1994;

Various Authors, *Le case coloniche/2, quaderno n°8 del Centro di Studi Chiantigiani "Clante"*, Poggibonsi 1996;

Various Authors, *Storia del vino in Toscana*, Firenze 2000;

A. Boglione, *Italiani e forestieri alla scoperta del Chianti*, in «Il Chianti», 18, Firenze 1995;

G. Brachetti Montorselli, I. Moretti, R. Stopani, *Le strade del Chianti (Il Gallo Nero)*, Firenze 1984;

A. Casabianca, *Guida storica del Chianti*, Firenze 1970;

E. Centri, *Discussione sul Chianti. Quello vero e quello inventato*, Firenze 1997;

G. Cherubini, *Il podere e la fattoria*, in Various Authors, *Una visione della Toscana. La terra, gli uomini, gli alimenti*, 1991;

R. Flower, *Chianti. Storia e cultura*, Firenze 1981;

L. Imbriani, *Guida ai migliori vini d'Italia*, Milano 1998;

I. Malenotti, *Manuale del vignaiolo toscano*, San Gimignano 2001;

F. Melis, *I vini italiani nel Medioevo*, Firenze 1984;

I. Moretti, *Qualche considerazione sulla nascita e sull'evoluzione del paesaggio chiantigiano*, in Various Authors, *Il paesaggio del Chianti: problemi e prospettive*, Firenze 1988;

E. Pellucci, G. Piscolla, *Vini di Toscana*, Firenze 1991;

G. Persichino, *Chianti Classico*, Firenze 2003;

P. Piussi, A. Zanzi Sulli, *Una storia dei boschi del Chianti*, in «Il Chianti», 17, Firenze 1994;

G. Sarrocchi, *Per il "Chianti del Chianti"*, Firenze 1942;

G. Sicheri, *Il libro completo del vino*, Novara 1988.

Index

This volume
was printed in Florence
for Nardini Editore
by Nuova Grafica Fiorentina
in the year 2005